Company's Coming

Stir-Fry

Jean Paré

companyscoming.com
visit our website

Front Cover

1. Curried Chicken, page 40
2. Blackened Shrimp, page 69
3. Avocado Chicken, page 43

Props Courtesy Of:
Clays Handmade Ceramic
Tile & Stone
Eaton's
The Bay

Back Cover

1. Chicken Penne, page 55
2. Ginger Pork And Peppers, page 95
3. Hot Lettuce Salad, page 101

Props Courtesy Of:
Clays Handmade
Ceramic Tile & Stone
Dansk Gifts
Eaton's
The Bay

Fifteenth Printing May 2004

Canadian Cataloguing in Publication Data

Paré, Jean
Stir-Fry

Includes index.
ISBN 1-895455-68-5

1. Entrées (Cookery). 1.Title.
TX693.P376 1999   641.8'1   C99-9001955-7

Published also in French under title: Les plats fricassés
ISBN 1-895455-70-7

Published by
Company's Coming Publishing Limited
2311 – 96 Street
Edmonton, Alberta, Canada T6N 1G3
Tel: 780-450-6223   Fax: 780-450-1857
www.companyscoming.com

Company's Coming is a registered trademark owned by
Company's Coming Publishing Limited

Printed in China

Visit us on-line

companyscoming.com

Who We Are | Browse Cookbooks | Cooking Tonight? | Home

everyday ingredients

feature recipes

feature recipes — Cooking tonight? Check out this month's ***feature recipes***—absolutely FREE!

tips and tricks — Looking for some great kitchen helpers? ***tips and tricks*** is here to save the day!

reader circle — In search of answers to cooking or household questions? Do you have answers you'd like to share? Join the fun with ***reader circle***, our on-line question and answer bulletin board. Great for swapping recipes too!

cooking links — Other interesting and informative web-sites are just a click away with ***cooking links.***

cookbook search — Find cookbooks by title, description or food category using ***cookbook search***.

e-mail us — We want to hear from you—***e-mail us*** lets you offer suggestions for upcoming titles, or share your favourite recipes.

Company's Coming
COOKBOOKS®

Canada's most popular cookbooks!

Company's Coming Cookbook Series

Original Series

- Softcover, 160 pages
- 6" x 9" (15 cm x 23 cm) format
- Lay-flat binding
- Full colour photos
- Nutrition information

Quick & easy recipes, everyday ingredients!

Lifestyle Series

- Softcover, 160 pages
- 8" x 10" (20 cm x 25 cm) format
- Paperback & spiral binding
- Full colour photos
- Nutrition information

Most Loved Recipe Collection

- Hardcover, 128 pages
- 8 3/4" x 8 3/4" (22 cm x 22 cm) format
- Full colour throughout
- Nutrition information

Special Occasion Series

- Hardcover & softcover, 192 pages
- 8 1/2" x 11" (22 cm x 28 cm) format
- Durable sewn binding
- Full colour throughout
- Nutrition information

See page 157 for a complete listing of cookbooks or visit companyscoming.com

Table of Contents

The Company's Coming Story

Jean Paré grew up understanding that the combination of family, friends and home cooking is the essence of a good life. From her mother she learned to appreciate good cooking, while her father praised even her earliest attempts. When she left home she took with her many acquired family recipes, a love of cooking and an intriguing desire to read recipe books like novels!

"never share a recipe you wouldn't use yourself"

In 1963, when her four children had all reached school age, Jean volunteered to cater the 50th anniversaryof the Vermilion School of Agriculture, now Lakeland College. Working out of her home, Jean prepared a dinner for over 1000 people which launched a flourishing catering operation that continued for over eighteen years. During that time she was provided with countless opportunities to test new ideas with immediate feedback—resulting in empty plates and contented customers! Whether preparing cocktail sandwiches for a house party or serving a hot meal for 1500 people, Jean Paré earned a reputation for good food, courteous service and reasonable prices.

"Why don't you write a cookbook?" Time and again, as requests for her recipes mounted, Jean was asked that question. Jean's response was to team up with her son, Grant Lovig, in the fall of 1980 to form Company's Coming Publishing Limited. April 14, 1981, marked the debut of "150 DELICIOUS SQUARES", the first Company's Coming cookbook in what soon would become Canada's most popular cookbook series.

Jean Paré's operation has grown steadily from the early days of working out of a spare bedroom in her home. Full-time staff includes marketing personnel located in major cities across Canada. Home Office is based in Edmonton, Alberta in a modern building constructed specially for the company.

Today the company distributes throughout Canada and the United States in addition to numerous overseas markets, all under the guidance of Jean's daughter, Gail Lovig. Best-sellers many times over in English, Company's Coming cookbooks have also been published in French and Spanish. Familiar and trusted in home kitchens around the world, Company's Coming cookbooks are offered in a variety of formats, including the original softcover series.

Jean Paré's approach to cooking has always called for quick and easy recipes using everyday ingredients. Even when travelling, she is constantly on the lookout for new ideas to share with her readers. At home, she can usually be found researching and writing recipes, or working in the company's test kitchen. Jean continues to gain new supporters by adhering to what she calls "the golden rule of cooking": never share a recipe you wouldn't use yourself. It's an approach that works—*millions of times over!*

Foreword

Stir-fry cooking is one of the most popular ways to cook today. Perhaps that's because stir-frying can be so fast and healthy!

The Chinese invented stir-frying hundreds of years ago when fuel for their cooking fires was in such short supply. They needed a way to prepare the food so it would cook quickly.

Traditionally, woks were used for stir-frying. However, the original style of wok with its rounded base is not as appropriate for use on today's flat stove top elements. That's why the newer style of wok with a flat bottom, or one with a supplementary ring for it to rest on, is the choice of most cooks. Although either a wok or frying pan can be used, the cone-design and high sides of a wok make the stirring and tossing technique more efficient—and you are more likely to keep the food in the pan!

One of the benefits of stir-frying is that it uses very little oil or fat; you need just enough oil or cooking spray to make a thin film in the pan. Stir-fry cooking is also a great way to include lots of different fresh vegetables in your family's daily diet. And because food cooks quickly, the nutrition content remains high.

Stir-Fry offers more than 150 kitchen-tested recipes with a wide variety of tastes, textures and colors. Among the many delicious selections in Stir-Fry you will find a special section that features more great ways to cook with a wok—soup-making and deep-frying.

So, gather your ingredients and get ready to stir-fry. For family or when company's coming, now you can be ready to feed them in a flash!

Jean Paré

Each recipe has been analyzed using the most up-to-date version of the Canadian Nutrient File from Health Canada, which is based on the United States Department of Agriculture (USDA) Nutrient Data Base. If more than one ingredient is listed (such as "hard margarine or butter"), or a range is given (1 – 2 tsp., 5 – 10 mL) then the first ingredient or amount is used in the analysis. Where an ingredient reads "sprinkle," "optional," or "for garnish," it is not included as part of the nutrition information. Milk, unless stated otherwise, is 1% and cooking oil, unless stated otherwise, is canola.

Margaret Ng, B.Sc. (Hon), M.A.
Registered Dietitian

getting started

Stir-fry is such a fast method of cooking. Have all the ingredients chopped, diced, cubed or slivered and waiting to be added. Mixing the sauce ahead is also a good idea.

Before starting to stir-fry, it is essential to know when to add which ingredients and approximately how long they should cook. Here's a quick guide for vegetable cooking times:

Longer Cooking (Firmer) Vegetables: Carrots, Cauliflower, Onions

Medium Cooking Vegetables: Cabbage, Asparagus, Peppers, Broccoli, Celery

Fast Cooking Vegetables: Pea Pods, Mushrooms, Green Onions, Tomatoes, Zucchini

The proper stir-fry technique is to use quick, downward strokes to keep the food in constant motion during the cooking process. In essence, the food should be constantly "stirred" while it is being "fried." Once they are ready, stir-fried foods shouldn't sit too long. Any accompanying side dishes such as salads, noodles or rice should be prepared and ready to serve as soon as the main stir-fry is done.

ingredients

Fish & Seafood: Stir-frying is a quick method to cook firm-fleshed fish and most seafood. Be careful though, because fish and seafood are easy to overcook and dry out. Have everything ready to serve just as soon as it's done.

Gingerroot: Simply slice about ⅛ inch (3 mm) thick pieces off the root, then chop into fine pieces. Using a fine grater works well too. It is not necessary to peel the root. Gingerroot offers a milder flavor than ground ginger.

Meat: The quick cooking time for stir-frying doesn't allow for tenderizing. Use tender cuts of meat such as beef tenderloin, beef top sirloin, beef rump steak, lean boneless pork loin or pork chops.

Oils: Cooking oils that can be heated to high temperatures without smoking are the preferred choice in stir-fry cooking. Vegetable oils are the most common. Oils such as peanut, corn, canola and sesame work well and subtly add different flavors to food. Try the following:

> *Hot Chili Oil:* Spicy hot oil made by steeping chili peppers. The resulting liquid is suspended in sesame or vegetable oil. It has a translucent red color and is excellent with most stir-fries where added "heat" is desired.

> *Sesame Oil:* Potent, flavorful oil extracted from sesame seeds that imparts a distinctive flavor to stir-fried meats and vegetables. It has a very good resistance to high heat and is excellent for deep-frying.

Pea Pods (Snow Peas/Chinese Pea Pods): A pea pod without the peas! To prepare, snap off, or cut off, the ends of the pod and remove the "string" that runs along its length. Both fresh and frozen (partially thawed under running water) work equally well.

Poultry: Boneless, skinless chicken breasts and thighs are a cook's answer to stir-fry. They are quick to cut, quick to cook, good with almost any sauce and any vegetable, and very low in fat. Though their initial price might seem higher than many meats, there is no waste and little fat making them a nutritional bargain!

Sauces: It's the sauce that makes the stir-fry! Becoming familiar with the different sauces and sauce ingredients is important. It's easy to create your own sauces by simply changing the amounts of one or several ingredients, or adding or subtracting one or more ingredients. The more popular sauces are:

Hoisin Sauce: A thick reddish sauce made from soybeans, garlic, chili peppers and a variety of spices. This sweet and spicy sauce is available at most grocery stores in a variety of brands.

Oyster Sauce: A thick, dark-brown, concentrated sauce made from oysters, brine and soy sauce and works well with meat, fish, poultry and vegetables. Oyster sauce is readily available at most grocery stores in a number of brands.

Soy Sauce: A thinner dark and salty sauce made by fermenting soybeans and roasted wheat or barley. Soy sauce is available in several varieties, including a low-sodium version, popular in today's health-conscious kitchens. Be careful not to add additional salt to a recipe until you have tasted the final result.

Tofu: This is commonly used as a substitute for meat by vegetarians and is a traditional Chinese ingredient used in stir-fry. Tofu offers no distinctive taste but has the ability to pick up the flavors of other foods. A firm tofu is recommended for stir-frying. Drain and cut about ¾ lb. (340 g) into ½ inch (12 mm) cubes before adding to wok.

Water Chestnuts: This is a white, nut-shaped vegetable most commonly found in canned form, either whole or sliced. This member of the chestnut family offers a wonderful crunchy texture to stir-fried food.

terminology

Chop: Cut food into bite-size, or smaller, pieces.

Dice: Cut food into ¼ inch (6 mm) cubes.

Cube: Cut food into ¾ inch (2 cm) cubes, or 1 inch (2.5 cm) cubes if you prefer larger pieces.

Strips: Cut food into long strips ⅛ to ¼ inch (3 to 6 mm) wide.

Slice: Vegetables that take the longest to cook are best cut diagonally into ⅛ inch (3 mm) thick slices. Other vegetables such as asparagus can be cut crosswise. When slicing meat, cut against the grain and remove all fat and sinew. Meat that is partially frozen will be easier to slice.

Autumn Stir-Fry

Nice autumn colors to this less common combination
of apple, onion and beef.

Prepared orange juice	¾ cup	175 mL
Cornstarch	1 tbsp.	15 mL
Water	1 tbsp.	15 mL
Brown sugar, packed	1 tbsp.	15 mL
Curry powder	2 tsp.	10 mL
Liquid beef bouillon	1 tsp.	5 mL
Cooking oil	1 tbsp.	15 mL
Sirloin steak, sliced into ⅛ inch (3 mm) thin strips	¾ lb.	340 g
Finely shredded cabbage	3 cups	750 mL
Cooking oil	1 tsp.	5 mL
Medium red pepper, cut into slivers	½	½
Chopped onion	½ cup	125 mL
Small cooking apple (such as Granny Smith), with peel, thinly sliced	1	1
Dark raisins	¼ cup	60 mL

Stir orange juice into cornstarch in small bowl. Add water, brown sugar, curry powder and beef bouillon. Stir. Set aside.

Heat wok or frying pan on medium-high. Add first amount of cooking oil. Add beef strips. Stir-fry until desired doneness. Transfer to bowl.

Add cabbage to hot wok. Stir-fry for 2 minutes until just wilted. Add to beef in bowl.

Add second amount of cooking oil to hot wok. Add remaining 4 ingredients. Stir-fry until onion is soft. Add beef mixture. Stir cornstarch mixture. Stir into beef mixture until boiling and thickened. Makes 4 cups (1 L). Serves 4.

1 serving: 252 Calories; 8.3 g Total Fat; 195 mg Sodium; 19 g Protein; 27 g Carbohydrate; 2 g Dietary Fiber

Pictured on page 53.

Beef

Beef Pizza Stir-Fry

A speedy meal to prepare. Not your usual stir-fry.

Elbow macaroni	2 cups	500 mL
Boiling water	3 qts.	3 L
Cooking oil (optional)	1 tbsp.	15 mL
Salt	2 tsp.	10 mL
Cooking oil	1 tbsp.	15 mL
Lean ground beef	¾ lb.	340 g
Small onion, chopped	1	1
Salt, sprinkle		
Pepper, sprinkle		
Sliced fresh mushrooms	2 cups	500 mL
Canned pizza sauce	7½ oz.	213 mL
Grated part-skim mozzarella cheese	1 cup	250 mL

Cook macaroni in boiling water, first amount of cooking oil and salt in large uncovered pot or Dutch oven for 5 to 7 minutes until tender but firm. Drain. Return macaroni to pot. Cover to keep warm.

Heat wok or frying pan on medium-high. Add second amount of cooking oil. Add ground beef and onion. Stir-fry until no pink remains in beef. Drain. Sprinkle with salt and pepper.

Add mushrooms. Stir-fry for 3 to 4 minutes until soft.

Stir in pizza sauce and macaroni. Stir until heated through.

Sprinkle with cheese or quickly stir cheese into hot mixture. Makes 3½ cups (875 mL). Serves 4.

1 serving: 495 Calories; 19 g Total Fat; 458 mg Sodium; 31 g Protein; 50 g Carbohydrate; 3 g Dietary Fiber

Paré Pointer

When Mutt and Jeff were lost, the police hunted high and low for them.

Beef Bourguignonne

A quick and easy method for the traditional recipe.

Water	¾ cup	175 mL
All-purpose flour	2 tbsp.	30 mL
Red (or alcohol-free red) wine	¼ cup	60 mL
Beef bouillon powder	1 tsp.	5 mL
Salt	½ tsp.	2 mL
Pepper	¼ tsp.	1 mL
Cooking oil	1 tbsp.	15 mL
Sirloin steak, sliced into ⅛ inch (3 mm) thin strips	½ lb.	225 g
Cooking oil	1 tsp.	5 mL
Tiny white pearl onions, peeled (see Note)	½ lb.	225 g
Fresh button mushrooms (or 10 oz., 284 mL, can, drained)	2 cups	500 mL

Gradually stir water into flour in small bowl until smooth. Mix in next 4 ingredients. Set aside.

Heat wok or frying pan on medium-high. Add first amount of cooking oil. Add beef strips. Stir-fry until desired doneness. Transfer to bowl.

Add second amount of cooking oil to hot wok. Add onions and mushrooms. Stir-fry for 3 minutes. Add beef. Stir flour mixture. Stir into beef mixture until boiling and thickened. Makes 3½ cups (875 mL). Serves 4.

1 serving: 163 Calories; 6.8 g Total Fat; 516 mg Sodium; 13 g Protein; 10 g Carbohydrate; 2 g Dietary Fiber

Pictured on page 36.

Note: To make peeling faster, boil onions in water for 5 minutes, drain, then plunge into ice water. Pinch at root end and onion should pop out of its skin.

Cook one pound or less of meat at a time to avoid the meat boiling in its own liquid. If liquid does form, turn heat up slightly and continue to stir-fry until all liquid is evaporated and meat is browned.

Veggie Beef

This stir-fry has just a hint of curry.

Low-sodium soy sauce	2 tsp.	10 mL
Cornstarch	1 tbsp.	15 mL
Oyster sauce	2 tsp.	10 mL
Apple juice	⅓ cup	75 mL
Chicken bouillon powder	1 tsp.	5 mL
Curry powder	¼ tsp.	1 mL
Ground ginger	¼ tsp.	1 mL
Cooking oil	1 tbsp.	15 mL
Sirloin steak, sliced into ⅛ inch (3 mm) thin strips	¾ lb.	340 g
Cooking oil	1 tsp.	5 mL
Small onion, sliced	1	1
Chopped or sliced celery	⅓ cup	75 mL
Medium green pepper, slivered	½	½
Medium red pepper, slivered	½	½
Medium yellow pepper, slivered	½	½
Garlic cloves, minced (or ½ tsp., 2 mL, powder)	2	2
Frozen pea pods, partially thawed (or 2 cups, 500 mL, fresh)	6 oz.	170 g

Stir soy sauce into cornstarch in small bowl. Add next 5 ingredients. Stir. Set aside.

Heat wok or frying pan on medium-high. Add first amount of cooking oil. Add beef strips. Stir-fry until desired doneness. Transfer to bowl.

Add second amount of cooking oil to hot wok. Add onion, celery, peppers, and garlic. Stir-fry for 3 minutes until vegetables are soft. Add to beef.

Stir-fry pea pods until tender-crisp. Add beef mixture. Stir cornstarch mixture. Stir into beef mixture until boiling and thickened. Makes 4 cups (1 L). Serves 4.

1 serving: 201 Calories; 8.1 g Total Fat; 534 mg Sodium; 19 g Protein; 13 g Carbohydrate; 2 g Dietary Fiber

Beef

Oriental Beef

Big pieces of beef, onion and broccoli.

Water	⅓ cup	75 mL
Cornstarch	2 tsp.	10 mL
Low-sodium soy sauce	1 tbsp.	15 mL
Sherry (or alcohol-free sherry)	2 tsp.	10 mL
Garlic powder	¼ tsp.	1 mL
Ground ginger	⅛ tsp.	0.5 mL
Beef bouillon powder	1 tsp.	5 mL
Salt	½ tsp.	2 mL
Pepper	⅛ tsp.	0.5 mL
Cooking oil	1 tbsp.	15 mL
Sirloin steak, sliced into ⅛ inch (3 mm) thin strips	¾ lb.	340 g
Small onion, cut into 6 wedges and layers separated	1	1
Broccoli florets	2 cups	500 mL
Water	2 tbsp.	30 mL

Stir first amount of water into cornstarch in small bowl. Add next 7 ingredients. Stir. Set aside.

Heat wok or frying pan on medium-high. Add cooking oil. Add beef strips and onion. Stir-fry for about 4 minutes until desired doneness. Transfer to bowl.

Add broccoli and second amount of water to hot wok. Cover. Steam for 3 minutes. Add beef mixture. Stir cornstarch mixture. Stir into beef mixture until boiling and thickened. Makes 3½ cups (875 mL). Serves 4.

1 serving: 162 Calories; 6.8 g Total Fat; 694 mg Sodium; 19 g Protein; 6 g Carbohydrate; 1 g Dietary Fiber

Pictured on page 71.

 tip *To keep gingerroot fresh for one to three weeks, wrap in a paper towel and refrigerate. It can also be frozen for several months to retain freshness longer.*

Mustard-Sauced Beef

Bright green and orange colors in this tasty dish.

Water	½ cup	125 mL
Cornstarch	1 tbsp.	15 mL
Beef bouillon powder	1½ tsp.	7 mL
Cooking oil	1 tbsp.	15 mL
Sirloin steak, sliced into ⅛ inch (3 mm) thin strips	¾ lb.	340 g
Salt, sprinkle		
Pepper, sprinkle		
Medium carrots, cut into thin sticks	2	2
Water	⅓ cup	75 mL
Fresh pea pods (or ½ x 6 oz., ½ x 170 g, frozen, partially thawed)	1 cup	250 mL
Mustard seed	½ tsp.	2 mL
Dried thyme	⅛ tsp.	0.5 mL

Stir first amount of water into cornstarch and bouillon powder in small bowl. Set aside.

Heat wok or frying pan on medium-high. Add cooking oil. Add beef strips. Stir-fry until desired doneness. Sprinkle with salt and pepper. Transfer to bowl.

Add carrot and second amount of water to hot wok. Reduce heat to medium. Cover. Steam for 5 minutes.

Add pea pods, mustard seed and thyme. Stir-fry for about 2 minutes. Add beef. Stir cornstarch mixture. Stir into beef mixture until boiling and thickened. Makes 3½ cups (875 mL). Serves 4.

1 serving: 176 Calories; 7 g Total Fat; 275 mg Sodium; 19 g Protein; 9 g Carbohydrate; 2 g Dietary Fiber

 To shorten stir-frying time, thaw frozen vegetables first by placing them in a colander, rinsing with hot water and draining well. It takes less than a minute!

Beef Muenster

Rich, spicy and cheesy. Serve over a bed of hot noodles.

Tomato sauce	7½ oz.	213 mL
Granulated sugar	1 tsp.	5 mL
Dried whole oregano	¼ tsp.	1 mL
Dried sweet basil	¼ tsp.	1 mL
Garlic powder	⅛ tsp.	0.5 mL
Salt	½ tsp.	2 mL
Pepper	⅛ tsp.	0.5 mL
Cooking oil	1 tbsp.	15 mL
Sirloin steak, sliced into ⅛ inch (3 mm) thin strips	¾ lb.	340 g
Grated Parmesan cheese	2 tbsp.	30 mL
Grated Muenster cheese	1 cup	250 mL

Measure first 7 ingredients into small bowl. Stir. Set aside.

Heat wok or frying pan on medium-high. Add cooking oil. Add beef strips. Stir-fry until desired doneness. Add tomato sauce mixture. Stir-fry until bubbling.

Stir in Parmesan cheese. Muenster cheese can either be stirred in or sprinkled over top. Makes 2 cups (500 mL). Serves 4.

1 serving: *273 Calories; 16.4 g Total Fat; 944 mg Sodium; 26 g Protein; 6 g Carbohydrate; 1 g Dietary Fiber*

1. Mangoes, page 58
2. Very Berry Banana, page 61

Props Courtesy Of: Chintz & Company
Le Gnome

Gingered Beef And Bok Choy

Serve immediately as the bok choy starts to wilt quickly.

Water	⅓ cup	75 mL
Cornstarch	1 tbsp.	15 mL
Sherry (or alcohol-free sherry)	2 tbsp.	30 mL
Low-sodium soy sauce	1 tbsp.	15 mL
Beef bouillon powder	1 tsp.	5 mL
Grated gingerroot	1 tbsp.	15 mL
Granulated sugar	1½ tsp.	7 mL
Salt	¼ tsp.	1 mL
Cooking oil	1 tbsp.	15 mL
Sirloin steak, sliced into ⅛ inch (3 mm) thin strips	¾ lb.	340 g
Chopped bok choy, packed	4 cups	1 L

Stir water into cornstarch in small bowl. Add next 6 ingredients. Stir. Set aside.

Heat wok or frying pan on medium-high. Add cooking oil. Add beef strips. Stir-fry until almost cooked. Stir cornstarch mixture. Stir into beef mixture until boiling and thickened.

Add bok choy. Stir until just starting to wilt. Makes 3 cups (750 mL). Serves 4.

1 serving: 165 Calories; 6.8 g Total Fat; 560 mg Sodium; 18 g Protein; 6 g Carbohydrate; 1 g Dietary Fiber

1. Beef And Zucchini, page 20

Props Courtesy Of: Chintz & Company
Salisbury Greenhouses
The Bay

Beef And Zucchini

To complete this fabulous dish, serve over hot noodles and add garlic toast.

Water	¼ cup	60 mL
Cornstarch	2 tsp.	10 mL
White vinegar	1 tbsp.	15 mL
Granulated sugar	½ tsp.	2 mL
Onion salt	⅛ tsp.	0.5 mL
Garlic salt	¼ tsp.	1 mL
Dried whole oregano	⅛ tsp.	0.5 mL
Ground thyme, just a pinch		
Olive (or cooking) oil	1 tbsp.	15 mL
Sirloin steak, sliced into ⅛ inch (3 mm) thin strips	¾ lb.	340 g
Salt, sprinkle		
Pepper, sprinkle		
Olive (or cooking) oil	1 tsp.	5 mL
Zucchini, 8 inches (20 cm) long, with peel, thinly sliced	1	1
Cherry tomatoes, halved	1 cup	250 mL
Grated Parmesan cheese, sprinkle (optional)		

Stir water into cornstarch in small bowl. Add next 6 ingredients. Stir. Set aside.

Heat wok or frying pan on medium-high. Add first amount of olive oil. Add beef strips. Stir-fry until desired doneness. Sprinkle with salt and pepper. Transfer to bowl.

Add second amount of olive oil to hot wok. Add zucchini. Stir-fry for 2 to 3 minutes until tender-crisp. Add beef.

Add tomato halves. Stir cornstarch mixture. Stir into beef mixture until boiling and thickened. Sprinkle with Parmesan cheese. Makes 3½ cups (875 mL). Serves 4.

1 serving: 160 Calories; 7.9 g Total Fat; 170 mg Sodium; 18 g Protein; 5 g Carbohydrate; 1 g Dietary Fiber

Pictured on page 18.

Beef, Broccoli And Pineapple

Add as much cayenne pepper as you like. It's not
too spicy but you know it's there.

Low-sodium soy sauce	2 tbsp.	30 mL
Cornstarch	2 tbsp.	30 mL
Oyster sauce	2 tsp.	10 mL
White vinegar	1½ tbsp.	25 mL
Reserved pineapple juice	¾ cup	175 mL
Cooking oil	1 tbsp.	15 mL
Sirloin steak, sliced into ⅛ inch (3 mm) thin strips	¾ lb.	340 g
Cayenne pepper	½ tsp.	2 mL
Cooking oil	1 tsp.	5 mL
Sliced broccoli (florets and peeled stems)	2 cups	500 mL
Small head of suey (or bok) choy, sliced	1	1
Canned pineapple tidbits, drained and juice reserved	14 oz.	398 mL
Sesame seeds, toasted	2 tbsp.	30 mL

Stir soy sauce into cornstarch in small bowl. Add next 3 ingredients. Stir. Set aside.

Heat wok or frying pan on medium-high. Add first amount of cooking oil. Add beef strips. Stir-fry until desired doneness. Sprinkle with cayenne pepper. Transfer to bowl.

Add second amount of cooking oil and broccoli to hot wok. Stir-fry for 3 minutes.

Add suey choy. Stir-fry for 1 minute. Add beef.

Add pineapple. Stir to heat through. Stir cornstarch mixture. Stir into beef mixture until boiling and thickened.

Sprinkle with sesame seeds. Makes 6 cups (1.5 L). Serves 6.

1 serving: 192 Calories; 7 g Total Fat; 409 mg Sodium; 14 g Protein; 20 g Carbohydrate; 3 g Dietary Fiber

Beef

Beef Mix

A meal in a hurry.

Lean ground beef	¾ lb.	340 g
Chopped onion	¼ cup	60 mL
Chopped green or orange pepper	3 tbsp.	50 mL
Tomato sauce	7½ oz.	213 mL
Instant rice	½ cup	125 mL
Canned kernel corn, drained	12 oz.	341 mL
Granulated sugar	½ tsp.	2 mL
Worcestershire sauce	½ tsp.	2 mL
Salt	1 tsp.	5 mL
Pepper	¼ tsp.	1 mL

Heat non-stick wok or frying pan on medium-high. Stir-fry ground beef, onion and green pepper until beef is no longer pink. Drain.

Add tomato sauce, rice, corn, sugar, Worcestershire sauce, salt, and pepper. Stir until boiling. Reduce heat to medium-low. Cover. Simmer for 5 minutes. Makes 4 cups (1 L). Serves 4.

1 serving: 248 Calories; 7.5 g Total Fat; 1216 mg Sodium; 19 g Protein; 28 g Carbohydrate; 2 g Dietary Fiber

Cashew Beef

Serve over hot basmati rice, or other. Cashews add a distinctive flavor.

Water	⅓ cup	75 mL
Cornstarch	1 tbsp.	15 mL
Beef bouillon powder	1 tsp.	5 mL
Low-sodium soy sauce	1 tbsp.	15 mL
Chili sauce	1 tsp.	5 mL
Garlic powder	¼ tsp.	1 mL
Ground ginger	⅛ tsp.	0.5 mL
Cooking oil	1 tbsp.	15 mL
Sirloin steak, sliced into ⅛ inch (3 mm) thin strips	¾ lb.	340 g
Frozen baby carrots, partially thawed	10 oz.	285 g
Water	2 tbsp.	30 mL
Green onions, sliced	3	3
Cashews	½ cup	125 mL

(continued on next page)

Beef

Stir first amount of water into cornstarch in small bowl. Add next 5 ingredients. Stir. Set aside.

Heat wok or frying pan on medium-high. Add cooking oil. Add beef strips. Stir-fry until desired doneness. Transfer to bowl.

Add carrots and second amount of water to hot wok. Cover. Steam for 5 minutes.

Add green onion and cashews. Stir-fry for 1 minute. Stir cornstarch mixture. Stir into vegetables until boiling and thickened. Add beef. Stir to heat through. Makes $3^2/_3$ cups (900 mL). Serves 4.

1 serving: 253 Calories; 15.1 g Total Fat; 349 mg Sodium; 20 g Protein; 10 g Carbohydrate; 1 g Dietary Fiber

Pictured on page 35.

Beefed Up Stir-Fry

Celery adds a nice crunch and bright green peas add to color and taste.

Ketchup	2 tbsp.	30 mL
Water	2 tbsp.	30 mL
Garlic powder	½ tsp.	2 mL
Worcestershire sauce	2 tsp.	10 mL
Envelope dry onion soup mix	1 x 1¼ oz.	1 x 38 g
Cooking oil	1 tbsp.	15 mL
Lean ground beef	¾ lb.	340 g
Finely chopped celery	1 cup	250 mL
Frozen peas	1 cup	250 mL
Instant rice	1 cup	250 mL
Boiling water	1 cup	250 mL

Measure first 5 ingredients into small bowl. Stir. Set aside.

Heat wok or frying pan on medium-high. Add cooking oil. Add ground beef and celery. Stir-fry for about 5 minutes until no pink remains in beef. Drain.

Add frozen peas. Stir-fry for about 1 minute. Add ketchup mixture. Stir for about 5 minutes until bubbling.

Add rice and boiling water. Cover. Remove from heat. Let stand for 5 to 7 minutes. Makes 3 cups (750 mL). Serves 4.

1 serving: 332 Calories; 11.3 g Total Fat; 1082 mg Sodium; 21 g Protein; 36 g Carbohydrate; 3 g Dietary Fiber

Beef

Far East Beef

Rich brown sauce over white noodles.

Rice vermicelli	3 oz.	85 g
Water		
Low-sodium soy sauce	2 tbsp.	30 mL
Cornstarch	2 tsp.	10 mL
White vinegar	1½ tbsp.	25 mL
Granulated sugar	1 tbsp.	15 mL
Dried crushed chilies	⅛ tsp.	0.5 mL
Cooking oil	1 tbsp.	15 mL
Sirloin steak, sliced into ⅛ inch (3 mm) thin strips	¾ lb.	340 g
Sliced onion	1 cup	250 mL
Grated gingerroot	2 tsp.	10 mL
Cooking oil	1 tsp.	5 mL
Red pepper slivers	½ cup	125 mL
Frozen green beans, partially thawed, cut into 1 inch (2.5 cm) lengths	1 cup	250 mL
Sliced fresh mushrooms	1 cup	250 mL
Fresh bean sprouts	3 cups	750 mL

Prepare vermicelli according to package directions. Drain. Cover to keep warm.

Stir soy sauce into cornstarch in cup. Add vinegar, sugar and crushed chilies. Stir. Set aside.

Heat wok or frying pan on medium-high. Add first amount of cooking oil. Add beef strips, onion and ginger. Stir-fry until beef is desired doneness and onion is soft. Transfer to bowl.

Add second amount of cooking oil to hot wok. Add red pepper slivers, green beans and mushrooms. Stir-fry for about 3 minutes. Add beef mixture.

Add bean sprouts. Stir cornstarch mixture. Stir into beef mixture until boiling and thickened. Makes 6 cups (1.5 L) without noodles. Pour over vermicelli. Serves 6.

1 serving: 222 Calories; 5.5 g Total Fat; 242 mg Sodium; 15 g Protein; 29 g Carbohydrate; 2 g Dietary Fiber

Pictured on page 71.

Beef

Beef And Spinach

A variety of colors and textures. Made with fresh spinach.

Low-sodium soy sauce	3 tbsp.	50 mL
Cornstarch	1 tsp.	5 mL
Granulated sugar	1 tsp.	5 mL
Ground ginger	1/4 tsp.	1 mL
Garlic powder	1/4 tsp.	1 mL
Dried crushed chilies	1/4 tsp.	1 mL
Fine egg noodles	8 oz.	225 g
Boiling water	2 1/2 qts.	2.5 L
Cooking oil (optional)	1 tbsp.	15 mL
Salt	2 tsp.	10 mL
Cooking oil	1 tbsp.	15 mL
Sirloin steak, sliced into 1/8 inch (3 mm) thin strips	3/4 lb.	340 g
Salt, sprinkle		
Pepper, sprinkle		
Cooking oil	1 tsp.	5 mL
Small red onion, sliced	1	1
Chopped fresh spinach, sliced, lightly packed	4 cups	1 L
Fresh bean sprouts	1 cup	250 mL
Ground nutmeg	1/4 tsp.	1 mL
Green onions, chopped	2	2

Stir soy sauce into cornstarch in cup. Add sugar, ginger, garlic powder and crushed chilies. Stir. Set aside.

Cook noodles in boiling water, first amount of cooking oil and salt in large uncovered pot or Dutch oven for 4 to 6 minutes until tender but firm. Drain. Return noodles to pot. Cover to keep warm.

Heat wok or frying pan on medium-high. Add second amount of cooking oil. Add beef strips. Stir-fry until desired doneness. Sprinkle with salt and pepper. Transfer to bowl.

Add third amount of cooking oil to hot wok. Add red onion. Stir fry for 2 minutes. Add spinach, bean sprouts and nutmeg. Stir-fry for 1 minute. Add beef and noodles. Stir to heat through.

Stir cornstarch mixture. Stir into beef mixture until boiling and thickened. Scatter green onion over top. Makes 7 cups (1.75 L). Serves 6.

1 serving: 267 Calories; 7 g Total Fat; 380 mg Sodium; 19 g Protein; 32 g Carbohydrate; 2 g Dietary Fiber

Beef

Saucy Ginger Beef

Dark, rich, thick sauce. Serve over a bed of hot rice. Delicious!

MARINADE

Low-sodium soy sauce	3 tbsp.	50 mL
Cornstarch	1 tbsp.	15 mL
Sherry (or alcohol-free sherry)	1 tbsp.	15 mL
Granulated sugar	1 tsp.	5 mL
Dried crushed chilies	¼ tsp.	1 mL
Ground ginger	¼ tsp.	1 mL
Garlic powder	¼ tsp.	1 mL
Salt	¼ tsp.	1 mL
Sirloin steak, sliced into ⅛ inch (3 mm) thin strips	¾ lb.	340 g
Water	¾ cup	175 mL
Cornstarch	1 tbsp.	15 mL
Cooking oil	1 tsp.	5 mL
Large onion, sliced	1	1
Granulated sugar	1 tsp.	5 mL
Cooking oil	1 tbsp.	15 mL
Green onions, sliced for garnish	2	2

Marinade: Stir soy sauce into first amount of cornstarch in medium bowl. Add next 6 ingredients. Stir.

Add beef strips. Cover. Marinate in refrigerator for 30 minutes.

Stir water into second amount of cornstarch in cup. Set aside.

Heat wok or frying pan on medium-high. Add first amount of cooking oil. Add onion. Stir-fry for 4 to 5 minutes.

Sprinkle with sugar. Stir-fry for 4 to 5 minutes until onion is golden.

Add second amount of cooking oil to onion. Remove beef with slotted spoon, reserving marinade. Add beef strips to hot wok. Stir-fry for 2 to 3 minutes until desired doneness. Add marinade. Stir cornstarch mixture. Stir into beef mixture until boiling and thickened.

Scatter green onion over top. Serves 4.

1 serving: 192 Calories; 7.8 g Total Fat; 680 mg Sodium; 19 g Protein; 11 g Carbohydrate; 1 g Dietary Fiber

Beef

Mediterranean Beef

Tender beef and herb-flavored vegetables. Tomatoes are the final touch.

Water	½ cup	125 mL
Cornstarch	1 tbsp.	15 mL
Dried whole oregano	½ tsp.	2 mL
Dried sweet basil	½ tsp.	2 mL
Beef bouillon powder	1 tsp.	5 mL
Salt	1 tsp.	5 mL
Pepper	1 tsp.	5 mL
Cooking oil	1 tbsp.	15 mL
Sirloin steak, sliced into ⅛ inch (3 mm) thin strips	¾ lb.	340 g
Cooking oil	1 tsp.	5 mL
Paper-thin carrot slices	½ cup	125 mL
Frozen cut green beans, partially thawed	½ cup	125 mL
Cooking oil	½ tsp.	2 mL
Thinly sliced zucchini, with peel	½ cup	125 mL
Sliced fresh mushrooms	1 cup	250 mL
Medium roma (plum) tomatoes, seeded and cubed	3	3
Grated Parmesan cheese, sprinkle		

Stir water into cornstarch in small bowl. Add next 5 ingredients. Stir. Set aside.

Heat wok or frying pan on medium-high. Add first amount of cooking oil. Add beef strips. Stir-fry for 1 to 2 minutes until desired doneness. Transfer to bowl.

Add second amount of cooking oil to hot wok. Add carrot and green beans. Stir-fry for 2 to 3 minutes. Transfer to bowl with beef.

Add third amount of cooking oil to hot wok. Add zucchini and mushrooms. Stir-fry for about 2 minutes. Add beef and vegetable mixture.

Add tomato. Stir cornstarch mixture. Stir into beef mixture until boiling and thickened.

Sprinkle with Parmesan cheese. Makes 4 cups (1 L). Serves 4.

1 serving: 188 Calories; 8.1 g Total Fat; 881 mg Sodium; 19 g Protein; 11 g Carbohydrate; 3 g Dietary Fiber

Pictured on page 72.

Beef And Bows

Add more dried crushed chilies to zip it up even more if you like.

Bow pasta	8 oz.	225 g
Boiling water	3 qts.	3 L
Cooking oil (optional)	1 tbsp.	15 mL
Salt	2 tsp.	10 mL
Cooking oil	1 tbsp.	15 mL
Sirloin steak, sliced into ⅛ inch (3 mm) thin strips	¾ lb.	340 g
Salt, sprinkle		
Pepper, sprinkle		
Cooking oil	1 tsp.	5 mL
Sliced fresh mushrooms	2 cups	500 mL
Medium red pepper, cut into ¾ inch (2 cm) squares	1	1
Dried crushed chilies	⅛ tsp.	0.5 mL
Grated Parmesan cheese	2 tbsp.	30 mL
Chopped fresh parsley	2 tbsp.	30 mL
Grated Parmesan cheese, sprinkle		

Cook pasta in boiling water, first amount of cooking oil and salt in large uncovered pot or Dutch oven for 12 to 14 minutes until tender but firm. Drain. Return bows to pot. Cover to keep warm.

Heat wok or frying pan on medium-high. Add second amount of cooking oil. Add beef strips. Stir-fry until desired doneness. Sprinkle with salt and pepper. Transfer to bowl.

Add third amount of cooking oil to hot wok. Add mushrooms, red pepper and crushed chilies. Stir-fry for 2 to 3 minutes until tender. Add beef. Heat through.

Add Parmesan cheese and parsley. Toss. Spread pasta on platter or 4 individual plates. Spoon beef mixture over top.

Sprinkle with Parmesan cheese. Serves 4.

1 serving: 379 Calories; 9.8 g Total Fat; 103 mg Sodium; 26 g Protein; 45 g Carbohydrate; 2 g Dietary Fiber

Pictured on page 35.

Beef

Beef And Broccoli

Wonderful mix of colors. Very showy!

Broad noodles	8 oz.	225 g
Boiling water	3 qts.	3 L
Cooking oil (optional)	1 tbsp.	15 mL
Salt	2 tsp.	10 mL
Water	½ cup	125 mL
Cornstarch	1 tbsp.	15 mL
Worcestershire sauce	1 tsp.	5 mL
Low-sodium soy sauce	2 tbsp.	30 mL
Cooking oil	1 tbsp.	15 mL
Sirloin steak, sliced into ⅛ inch (3 mm) thin strips	¾ lb.	340 g
Garlic clove, minced (or ¼ tsp., 1 mL, powder), optional	1	1
Cooking oil	1 tsp.	5 mL
Broccoli florets	1 cup	250 mL
Sliced fresh mushrooms	1 cup	250 mL
Canned sliced water chestnuts, drained	8 oz.	227 mL
Cherry tomatoes, halved	12	12
Sliced or chopped pimiento	2 oz.	57 mL

Cook noodles in boiling water, first amount of cooking oil and salt in large uncovered pot or Dutch oven for 5 to 7 minutes until tender but firm. Drain. Return noodles to pot. Cover to keep warm.

Stir water into cornstarch in small bowl. Stir in Worcestershire sauce and soy sauce. Set aside.

Heat wok or frying pan on medium-high. Add second amount of cooking oil. Add beef strips and garlic. Stir-fry for 3 to 4 minutes until desired doneness. Transfer to bowl.

Add third amount of cooking oil to hot wok. Add broccoli, mushrooms and water chestnuts. Stir-fry for about 3 minutes. Add beef mixture.

Add tomato halves and pimiento. Stir cornstarch mixture. Stir into beef mixture until boiling and thickened. Spread noodles on platter or 4 individual plates. Spoon beef mixture over top. Serves 4.

1 serving: 412 Calories; 9 g Total Fat; 386 mg Sodium; 27 g Protein; 55 g Carbohydrate; 3 g Dietary Fiber

Beef And Green Beans

Whole green beans make this an attractive dish.

Low-sodium soy sauce	2 tbsp.	30 mL
Cornstarch	1 tbsp.	15 mL
Water	¼ cup	60 mL
Granulated sugar	1 tsp.	5 mL
Worcestershire sauce	1 tsp.	5 mL
Prepared orange juice	1 tbsp.	15 mL
Seasoned salt	½ tsp.	2 mL
Cooking oil	1 tbsp.	15 mL
Sirloin steak, sliced into ⅛ inch (3 mm) thin strips	¾ lb.	340 g
Slivered red onion	½ cup	125 mL
Whole frozen green beans, partially thawed	1 lb.	454 g
Salt, sprinkle		
Pepper, sprinkle		

Stir soy sauce into cornstarch in small bowl. Add next 5 ingredients. Stir. Set aside.

Heat wok or frying pan on medium-high. Add cooking oil. Add beef strips and onion. Stir-fry until beef is desired doneness and onion is soft. Transfer to bowl.

Add green beans to hot wok. Stir-fry until tender-crisp. Add beef. Sprinkle with salt and pepper. Stir cornstarch mixture. Stir into beef mixture until boiling and thickened. Makes 6 cups (1.5 L). Serves 6.

1 serving: 125 Calories; 4.5 g Total Fat; 367 mg Sodium; 13 g Protein; 9 g Carbohydrate; 2 g Dietary Fiber

Pictured on page 36.

 tip   *There probably isn't a more flexible method of cooking than stir-fry. Don't have the box of frozen pea pods in the freezer that you thought you did? Just add more of one of the other vegetables listed in the recipe—or choose an additional one. Just try to keep the total amount the same.*

Beef

Beef Stroganoff

Definitely stroganoff! Lots of sauce. Such a comforting dish.

Broad noodles	8 oz.	225 g
Boiling water	3 qts.	3 L
Cooking oil (optional)	1 tbsp.	15 mL
Salt	2 tsp.	10 mL
Water	½ cup	125 mL
All-purpose flour	1½ tbsp.	25 mL
Beef bouillon powder	2 tsp.	10 mL
Cooking oil	1 tbsp.	15 mL
Sirloin steak, sliced into ⅛ inch (3 mm) thin strips	¾ lb.	340 g
Salt, sprinkle		
Pepper, sprinkle		
Cooking oil	1 tsp.	5 mL
Sliced onion	½ cup	125 mL
Small fresh mushrooms, halved	2 cups	500 mL
Low-fat sour cream	¼ cup	60 mL
Green onion, sliced	1	1

Cook noodles in boiling water, first amount of cooking oil and salt in large uncovered pot or Dutch oven for 5 to 7 minutes until tender but firm. Drain. Return noodles to pot. Cover to keep warm.

Gradually stir water into flour and bouillon powder in small bowl until smooth. Set aside.

Heat wok or frying pan on medium-high. Add second amount of cooking oil. Add beef strips. Stir-fry until desired doneness. Sprinkle with salt and pepper. Transfer to bowl.

Add third amount of cooking oil to hot wok. Add onion and mushrooms. Stir-fry until golden. Add beef. Stir in flour mixture until boiling and thickened.

Mix in sour cream. Serve over noodles. Scatter green onion over top. Serves 4.

1 serving: 396 Calories; 10 g Total Fat; 347 mg Sodium; 26 g Protein; 49 g Carbohydrate; 2 g Dietary Fiber

Cupboard Stir-Fry

Very tasty! Very quick! Even faster
if you keep beef strips handy in the freezer.

Broad noodles	8 oz.	225 g
Boiling water	3 qts.	3 L
Cooking oil (optional)	1 tbsp.	15 mL
Salt	2 tsp.	10 mL
Cooking oil	1 tbsp.	15 mL
Sirloin steak, sliced into 1/8 inch (3 mm) thin strips	3/4 lb.	340 g
Salt, sprinkle		
Pepper, sprinkle		
Canned stewed tomatoes, with juice	14 oz.	398 mL
Canned mixed vegetables, drained	14 oz.	398 mL
Canned sliced mushrooms, drained	10 oz.	284 mL
Dried whole oregano	1/2 tsp.	2 mL
Dried sweet basil	1/2 tsp.	2 mL
Granulated sugar	1/2 tsp.	2 mL
Onion powder	1/4 tsp.	1 mL
Cornstarch	2 tsp.	10 mL

Cook noodles in boiling water, first amount of cooking oil and salt in large uncovered pot or Dutch oven for 5 to 7 minutes until tender but firm. Drain. Return noodles to pot. Cover to keep warm.

Heat wok or frying pan on medium-high. Add second amount of cooking oil. Add beef strips. Stir-fry for 4 to 5 minutes until desired doneness. Sprinkle with salt and pepper.

Add remaining 8 ingredients. Stir until boiling and thickened. Spread noodles on platter or 4 individual plates. Spoon beef mixture over top. Serves 4.

1 serving: 420 Calories; 8 g Total Fat; 693 mg Sodium; 27 g Protein; 60 g Carbohydrate; 6 g Dietary Fiber

Beef

Shredded Stew

A nice mix of colors. Serve over hot potatoes, rice or noodles.

Water	⅓ cup	75 mL
Cornstarch	1 tbsp.	15 mL
Oyster sauce	3 tbsp.	50 mL
Sherry (or alcohol-free sherry)	1 tbsp.	15 mL
Beef bouillon powder	1 tsp.	5 mL
Low-sodium soy sauce	½ tsp.	2 mL
Salt	¼ tsp.	1 mL
Cooking oil	1 tbsp.	15 mL
Sirloin steak, sliced into ⅛ inch (3 mm) thin strips	¾ lb.	340 g
Garlic clove, minced (or ¼ tsp., 1 mL, powder)	1	1
Cooking oil	1 tsp.	5 mL
Medium carrots, shredded	2	2
Medium zucchini, with peel, cut into matchsticks	1	1
Chopped bok choy, packed	1 cup	250 mL
Small red pepper, cut into matchsticks	1	1
Fresh bean sprouts	1 cup	250 mL

Stir water into cornstarch in small bowl. Add next 5 ingredients. Stir. Set aside.

Heat wok or frying pan on medium-high. Add first amount of cooking oil. Add beef strips and garlic. Stir-fry for about 3 minutes until desired doneness. Transfer to bowl.

Add second amount of cooking oil to hot wok. Add carrot. Stir-fry for 2 minutes. Add zucchini, bok choy, red pepper and bean sprouts. Stir-fry for 2 minutes. Add beef. Stir cornstarch mixture. Stir into beef mixture until boiling and thickened. Makes 4 cups (1 L). Serves 4.

1 serving: 208 Calories; 8.1 g Total Fat; 1487 mg Sodium; 19 g Protein; 14 g Carbohydrate; 2 g Dietary Fiber

Beef In Oyster Sauce

A dark brown glossy sauce. Looks and tastes rich.

Water	1 tbsp.	15 mL
Cornstarch	1 tbsp.	15 mL
Oyster sauce	3 tbsp.	50 mL
Low-sodium soy sauce	1 tbsp.	15 mL
Sherry (or alcohol-free sherry)	2 tsp.	10 mL
Salt	¼ tsp.	1 mL
Ground ginger	¼ tsp.	1 mL
Cooking oil	1 tbsp.	15 mL
Sirloin steak, sliced into ⅛ inch (3 mm) thin strips	¾ lb.	340 g
Small fresh mushrooms	12	12
Canned bamboo shoots, drained	8 oz.	227 mL

Stir water into cornstarch in small bowl. Add next 5 ingredients. Stir. Set aside.

Heat wok or frying pan on medium-high. Add cooking oil. Add beef strips. Stir-fry until desired doneness.

Add mushrooms and bamboo shoots. Stir-fry for 5 minutes until mushrooms are soft. Stir cornstarch mixture. Stir into beef mixture until boiling and thickened. Serves 4.

1 serving: 170 Calories; 6.9 g Total Fat; 1447 mg Sodium; 18 g Protein; 8 g Carbohydrate; trace Dietary Fiber

1. Champagne Chicken, page 46
2. Cashew Beef, page 22
3. Beef And Bows, page 28

Props Courtesy Of: Chintz & Company
The Bay

Beefy Vegetables

Very colorful! Sauce gives a glossy coat.

Water	½ cup	125 mL
Cornstarch	1 tbsp.	15 mL
Low-sodium soy sauce	2 tbsp.	30 mL
Granulated sugar	½ tsp.	2 mL
Ground ginger	½ tsp.	2 mL
Garlic powder	½ tsp.	2 mL
Salt, sprinkle		
Cooking oil	2 tsp.	10 mL
Sirloin steak, sliced into ⅛ inch (3 mm) thin strips	¾ lb.	340 g
Frozen California mixed vegetables (including broccoli and cauliflower), partially thawed	32 oz.	900 g
Fresh pea pods (or 6 oz., 170 g, frozen, partially thawed)	2 cups	500 mL
Water	½ cup	125 mL

Stir first amount of water into cornstarch in small bowl. Add next 5 ingredients. Stir. Set aside.

Heat wok or frying pan on medium-high. Add cooking oil. Add beef strips. Stir-fry for 3 minutes until desired doneness. Transfer to bowl.

Add vegetables and second amount of water to hot wok. Reduce heat. Cover. Steam for 3 minutes. Remove cover. Increase heat. Stir-fry for 2 minutes. Add beef. Stir cornstarch mixture. Stir into beef mixture until boiling and thickened. Makes 5 cups (1.25 L). Serves 4.

1 serving: 288 Calories; 5.8 g Total Fat; 430 mg Sodium; 25 g Protein; 36 g Carbohydrate; 10 g Dietary Fiber

1. Beef Bourguignonne, page 12
2. Beef And Green Beans, page 30

Props Courtesy Of: Chintz & Company
Le Gnome
The Bay

Beef Broccoli

Always a hit. Colorful with a glossy sauce.

Low-sodium soy sauce	1 tbsp.	15 mL
Cornstarch	1 tsp.	5 mL
Sherry (or alcohol-free sherry)	1 tbsp.	15 mL
Oyster sauce	2 tbsp.	30 mL
Salt	1/2 tsp.	2 mL
Pepper	1/4 tsp.	1 mL
Cooking oil	1 tsp.	5 mL
Sliced broccoli (florets and peeled stems)	3 cups	750 mL
Cooking oil	1 tbsp.	15 mL
Sirloin steak, sliced into 1/8 inch (3 mm) thin strips	3/4 lb.	340 g

Stir soy sauce into cornstarch in small cup. Add next 4 ingredients. Stir. Set aside.

Heat wok or frying pan on medium-high. Add first amount of cooking oil. Add broccoli. Stir-fry for 4 minutes until tender-crisp. Transfer to bowl.

Add second amount of cooking oil to hot wok. Add beef strips. Stir-fry until desired doneness. Add broccoli. Stir cornstarch mixture. Stir into beef mixture until boiling and thickened. Makes 3 1/2 cups (875 mL). Serves 4.

1 serving: 184 Calories; 8.6 g Total Fat; 1273 mg Sodium; 19 g Protein; 7 g Carbohydrate; 2 g Dietary Fiber

Chili Beef Stir-Fry

A fast way to make chili! Goes further if served over hot rice.

Cooking oil	1 tsp.	5 mL
Lean ground beef	3/4 lb.	340 g
Cooking oil	1 tsp.	5 mL
Large onion, sliced or chopped	1	1
Chili powder	2 tsp.	10 mL
Seasoned salt	1/2 tsp.	2 mL
Cayenne pepper	1/8 tsp.	0.5 mL
Canned diced tomatoes, drained and 1/4 cup (60 mL) juice reserved	14 oz.	398 mL
Canned kidney beans, drained	14 oz.	398 mL
Granulated sugar	1 tsp.	5 mL
Reserved juice from tomatoes		

(continued on next page)

Heat wok or frying pan on medium-high. Add first amount of cooking oil. Add ground beef. Stir-fry until beef is no longer pink. Drain. Transfer to bowl.

Add second amount of cooking oil to hot wok. Add onion, chili powder, seasoned salt and cayenne pepper. Stir-fry for about 2 minutes until onion is browned. Add beef. Stir.

Add tomatoes, kidney beans, sugar and reserved juice from tomatoes. Stir until mixture comes to a boil. Makes 6 cups (1.5 L). Serves 4.

1 serving: 347 Calories; 16 g Total Fat; 530 mg Sodium; 29 g Protein; 22 g Carbohydrate; 6 g Dietary Fiber

Mandarin Beef

Sauce is spicy and sweet—very appealing! Serve over hot rice or noodles.

Low-sodium soy sauce	2 tbsp.	30 mL
Cornstarch	4 tsp.	20 mL
Oyster sauce	1 tbsp.	15 mL
Sherry (or alcohol-free sherry)	1 tbsp.	15 mL
White vinegar	1 tbsp.	15 mL
Granulated sugar	1 tbsp.	15 mL
Ketchup	1½ tsp.	7 mL
Garlic powder	¼ tsp.	1 mL
Cooking oil	1 tbsp.	15 mL
Sirloin steak, sliced into ⅛ inch (3 mm) thin strips	¾ lb.	340 g
Green onions, halved lengthwise and cut into 2 inch (5 cm) lengths	4	4
Toasted sesame seeds, for garnish	1 tsp.	5 mL

Stir soy sauce into cornstarch in small cup. Add next 6 ingredients. Stir. Set aside.

Heat wok or frying pan on medium-high. Add cooking oil. Add beef strips. Stir-fry until no pink remains in beef.

Add green onion. Stir-fry until soft. Stir cornstarch mixture. Stir into beef mixture until boiling and thickened. Sprinkle with sesame seeds. Makes 2 cups (500 mL). Serves 4.

1 serving: 171 Calories; 6.6 g Total Fat; 736 mg Sodium; 18 g Protein; 9 g Carbohydrate; trace Dietary Fiber

Pictured on page 107.

Curried Chicken

A hint of curry but not overbearing. A flavorful, attractive dish.

Long grain white (or basmati) rice	1⅓ cups	325 mL
Water	2⅔ cups	650 mL
Salt	½ tsp.	2 mL
White (or alcohol-free white) wine	½ cup	125 mL
Cornstarch	2 tsp.	10 mL
Cooking oil	1 tbsp.	15 mL
Boneless, skinless chicken breast halves (about 4), cut bite size	1 lb.	454 g
Chopped onion	½ cup	125 mL
Medium cooking apple (such as McIntosh), with peel, chopped	1	1
Raisins	⅓ cup	75 mL
Curry powder	1 tsp.	5 mL
Brown sugar, packed	2 tsp.	10 mL
Ground thyme	¼ tsp.	1 mL
Poultry seasoning	½ tsp.	2 mL
Salt	¼ tsp.	1 mL
Pepper, just a pinch		

Cook rice in water and first amount of salt in medium saucepan for 15 to 20 minutes until tender and water is absorbed.

Stir wine into cornstarch in small bowl. Set aside.

Heat wok or frying pan on medium-high. Add cooking oil. Add chicken and onion. Stir-fry until no pink remains in chicken. Transfer to bowl.

Combine remaining 8 ingredients in hot wok. Stir-fry until apple is tender. Add chicken mixture. Stir to heat through. Stir cornstarch mixture. Stir into chicken mixture until boiling and thickened. Makes 4 cups (1 L). Spread rice on platter or 4 individual plates. Spoon chicken mixture over rice. Serves 4.

1 serving: 517 Calories; 6.7 g Total Fat; 256 mg Sodium; 33 g Protein; 77 g Carbohydrate; 4 g Dietary Fiber

Pictured on front cover.

Chicken

Sherried Chicken

A straight forward stir-fry. Makes a nice company dish.

Condensed chicken broth	½ x 10 oz.	½ x 284 mL
Cornstarch	1 tbsp.	15 mL
Milk	2 tbsp.	30 mL
Salt	⅛ tsp.	0.5 mL
Pepper	⅛ tsp.	0.5 mL
Cooking oil	1 tbsp.	15 mL
Boneless, skinless chicken breast halves (about 3), cut into thin strips	¾ lb.	340 g
Onion slivers	1 cup	250 mL
Cooking oil	1 tsp.	5 mL
Medium carrots, cut julienne	2	2
Diagonally sliced celery	½ cup	125 mL
Slivered green pepper	½ cup	125 mL
Sherry (or alcohol-free sherry)	1 tbsp.	15 mL

Grated Parmesan cheese, sprinkle

Stir chicken broth into cornstarch in small bowl. Add next 3 ingredients. Stir. Set aside.

Heat wok or frying pan on medium-high. Add first amount of cooking oil. Add chicken strips and onion. Stir-fry until no pink remains in chicken and onion is soft. Transfer to bowl.

Add second amount of cooking oil to hot wok. Add carrot and celery. Stir-fry for 2 to 3 minutes until tender-crisp.

Add green pepper. Stir-fry for about 1 minute. Stir cornstarch mixture. Stir into vegetable mixture until boiling and thickened. Add chicken mixture.

Add sherry. Stir to heat through.

Sprinkle with Parmesan cheese. Serves 4.

1 serving: 200 Calories; 6.3 g Total Fat; 413 mg Sodium; 23 g Protein; 12 g Carbohydrate; 2 g Dietary Fiber

Almond Chicken

Almonds, bean sprouts and water chestnuts all add crunch.

Long grain white rice	1⅓ cups	325 mL
Water	2⅔ cups	650 mL
Salt	½ tsp.	2 mL
Water	½ cup	125 mL
Cornstarch	1 tbsp.	15 mL
Low-sodium soy sauce	2 tbsp.	30 mL
Chicken bouillon powder	1 tsp.	5 mL
Cooking oil	1 tbsp.	15 mL
Boneless, skinless chicken breast halves (about 3), cut bite size	¾ lb.	340 g
Diagonally sliced celery	1 cup	250 mL
Cooking oil	1 tsp.	5 mL
Sliced fresh mushrooms	1 cup	250 mL
Fresh bean sprouts	2 cups	500 mL
Canned sliced water chestnuts, drained	8 oz.	227 mL
Slivered almonds, toasted	½ cup	125 mL

Cook rice in first amount of water and salt in medium saucepan for 15 to 20 minutes until tender and water is absorbed.

Stir second amount of water into cornstarch in small bowl. Add soy sauce and bouillon powder. Stir. Set aside.

Heat wok or frying pan on medium-high. Add first amount of cooking oil. Add chicken and celery. Stir-fry for about 4 minutes until no pink remains in chicken. Transfer to bowl.

Add second amount of cooking oil to hot wok. Add mushrooms, bean sprouts and water chestnuts. Stir-fry for about 2 minutes until mushrooms are soft and moisture is evaporated. Add chicken and celery. Stir cornstarch mixture. Stir into chicken mixture until boiling and thickened. Makes 6 cups (1.5 L). Spread rice on platter or 4 individual plates. Spoon chicken mixture over top.

Sprinkle with almonds. Serves 4.

1 serving: 538 Calories; 15.7 g Total Fat; 571 mg Sodium; 31 g Protein; 69 g Carbohydrate; 5 g Dietary Fiber

Chicken

Avocado Chicken

If you have never cooked with avocado, this is an ideal way to start.

Water	½ cup	125 mL
Cornstarch	1 tbsp.	15 mL
Lemon juice	1 tsp.	5 mL
Chicken bouillon powder	1 tsp.	5 mL
Cooking oil	1 tbsp.	15 mL
Boneless, skinless chicken breast halves (about 3), cut bite size	¾ lb.	340 g
Cooking oil	1 tsp.	5 mL
Red pepper chunks	½ cup	125 mL
Sliced fresh mushrooms	1 cup	250 mL
Curry powder	2 tsp.	10 mL
Salt	¼ tsp.	1 mL
Pepper	¼ tsp.	1 mL
Firm ripe avocado, peeled and sliced	1	1
Sesame seeds, toasted	1 tbsp.	15 mL

Stir water into cornstarch in small bowl. Add lemon juice and bouillon powder. Stir. Set aside.

Heat wok or frying pan on medium-high. Add first amount of cooking oil. Add chicken. Stir-fry until no pink remains in chicken. Transfer to bowl.

Add second amount of cooking oil to hot wok. Add red pepper chunks, mushrooms, curry powder, salt and pepper. Stir-fry for about 2 minutes until moisture is evaporated. Add chicken.

Add avocado. Stir-fry for about 1 minute. Stir cornstarch mixture. Stir into chicken mixture until boiling and thickened.

Sprinkle with sesame seeds. Serves 4.

1 serving: 251 Calories; 14.9 g Total Fat; 395 mg Sodium; 22 g Protein; 9 g Carbohydrate; 2 g Dietary Fiber

Pictured on front cover.

Chicken Chow Mein

A dark-colored sauce that coats the chicken and vegetables nicely.

Condensed chicken broth	10 oz.	284 mL
Cornstarch	2 tbsp.	30 mL
Fancy molasses	2 tbsp.	30 mL
Low-sodium soy sauce	3 tbsp.	50 mL
Short grain white rice	1¼ cups	300 mL
Water	2½ cups	625 mL
Salt	½ tsp.	2 mL
Cooking oil	1 tbsp.	15 mL
Boneless, skinless chicken breast halves (about 3), cut into thin strips	¾ lb.	340 g
Cooking oil	1 tsp.	5 mL
Small green pepper, cut into slivers	1	1
Chopped onion	1 cup	250 mL
Chopped celery	½ cup	125 mL
Fresh bean sprouts	2 cups	500 mL
Canned sliced water chestnuts, drained	8 oz.	227 mL
Canned bamboo shoots, drained	8 oz.	227 mL
Canned sliced mushrooms, drained	10 oz.	284 mL
Chow mein noodles	1 cup	250 mL

Stir chicken broth into cornstarch in small bowl. Add molasses and soy sauce. Stir. Set aside.

Cook rice in water and salt in large covered saucepan for 15 to 20 minutes until tender and water is absorbed. Remove from heat. Cover to keep warm.

Heat wok or frying pan on medium-high. Add first amount of cooking oil. Add chicken strips. Stir-fry for 4 to 5 minutes until no pink remains in chicken. Transfer to bowl.

Add second amount of cooking oil to hot wok. Add green pepper, onion and celery. Stir-fry for 3 to 5 minutes until soft.

Add bean sprouts. Stir-fry for 1 minute.

(continued on next page)

Chicken

Add water chestnuts, bamboo shoots and mushrooms. Stir-fry until hot. Add chicken. Stir cornstarch mixture. Stir into chicken mixture until boiling and thickened. Serve over rice. Sprinkle with noodles. Serves 4.

1 serving: 575 Calories; 10.4 g Total Fat; 1224 mg Sodium; 33 g Protein; 88 g Carbohydrate; 5 g Dietary Fiber

Shrimp Chow Mein: Omit chicken. Use ¾ lb. (340 g) fresh raw medium shrimp, peeled and deveined. Stir-fry until pinkish and curled.

Chicken And Mushrooms

Very quick to prepare. Serve over hot fettuccine or linguine.

Skim evaporated milk	½ cup	125 mL
Cornstarch	2 tsp.	10 mL
Chicken bouillon powder	1 tsp.	5 mL
Salt	¼ tsp.	1 mL
Pepper	¼ tsp.	1 mL
Paprika	¼ tsp.	1 mL
Cooking oil	1 tbsp.	15 mL
Boneless, skinless chicken breast halves (about 3), cut into thin strips	¾ lb.	340 g
Chopped onion	¼ cup	60 mL
Sliced fresh mushrooms	2 cups	500 mL
Frozen peas	1 cup	250 mL
White (or alcohol-free white) wine	4 tsp.	20 mL

Stir evaporated milk into cornstarch in small bowl. Add next 4 ingredients. Stir. Set aside.

Heat wok or frying pan on medium-high. Add cooking oil. Add chicken strips and onion. Stir-fry until no pink remains in chicken. Transfer to bowl.

Add mushrooms and frozen peas to hot wok. Stir-fry for about 2 minutes until mushrooms are soft and moisture is evaporated. Add chicken mixture. Stir cornstarch mixture. Stir into chicken mixture until boiling and thickened.

Stir in wine. Serves 4.

1 serving: 205 Calories; 5 g Total Fat; 471 mg Sodium; 25 g Protein; 13 g Carbohydrate; 2 g Dietary Fiber

Champagne Chicken

Make this when peaches are at their best.

Champagne (or ginger ale)	1/3 cup	75 mL
Cornstarch	2 tsp.	10 mL
Medium noodles	2 cups	500 mL
Boiling water	2 1/2 qts.	2.5 L
Cooking oil (optional)	1 tbsp.	15 mL
Salt	2 tsp.	10 mL
Cooking oil	1 tbsp.	15 mL
Boneless, skinless chicken breast halves (about 4), cut into thin strips	1 lb.	454 g
Chopped onion	1/4 cup	60 mL
Fresh peaches, peeled and sliced (see Note)	2	2
Green onions, sliced	2	2
Granulated sugar	2 tsp.	10 mL
Lemon juice	1 tbsp.	15 mL
Salt	1/4 tsp.	1 mL
Pepper	1/4 tsp.	1 mL

Stir champagne into cornstarch in small bowl. Set aside.

Cook noodles in boiling water and first amounts of cooking oil and salt in large uncovered pot or Dutch oven for 5 to 7 minutes until tender but firm. Drain. Return noodles to pot. Cover to keep warm.

Heat wok or frying pan on medium-high. Add second amount of cooking oil. Add chicken strips and onion. Stir-fry until no pink remains in chicken. Transfer to bowl.

Add peach slices, green onion, sugar, lemon juice, second amount of salt and pepper to hot wok. Stir-fry for 1 1/2 to 2 minutes until soft. Add chicken and noodles. Stir cornstarch mixture. Stir into chicken mixture until boiling and thickened. Serve immediately as peaches will darken. Makes 4 cups (1 L). Serves 4.

1 serving: 372 Calories; 5.6 g Total Fat; 248 mg Sodium; 32 g Protein; 43 g Carbohydrate; 2 g Dietary Fiber

Pictured on page 35.

Note: To peel peaches, plunge into bowl of boiling water for about 1 minute. Remove carefully with tongs and peel with paring knife.

Chicken And Broccoli

Contains chicken and vegetables. Serve with hot rice for a balanced meal.

Water	½ cup	125 mL
Cornstarch	2 tbsp.	30 mL
Cooking oil	1 tbsp.	15 mL
Boneless, skinless chicken breast halves (about 4), cut into thin strips	1 lb.	454 g
Thinly sliced onion	1 cup	250 mL
Thinly sliced carrot	1 cup	250 mL
Cooking oil	1 tsp.	5 mL
Small bite-size broccoli pieces	2 cups	500 mL
Low-sodium soy sauce	¼ cup	60 mL
Chicken bouillon powder	2 tsp.	10 mL
Sherry (or alcohol-free sherry)	1 tbsp.	15 mL
Garlic powder	¼ tsp.	1 mL
Ground ginger	⅛ tsp.	0.5 mL
Sliced almonds, toasted (optional)	½ cup	125 mL

Stir water into cornstarch in small bowl. Set aside.

Heat wok or frying pan on medium-high. Add first amount of cooking oil. Add chicken strips, onion and carrot. Stir-fry for about 4 minutes until no pink remains in chicken.

Add second amount of cooking oil to hot wok. Add broccoli. Stir fry for 3 minutes until bright green.

Add remaining 6 ingredients. Stir to heat through. Stir cornstarch mixture. Stir into chicken mixture until boiling and thickened. Makes 4 cups (1 L). Serves 4.

1 serving: 242 Calories; 6.4 g Total Fat; 1081 mg Sodium; 30 g Protein; 15 g Carbohydrate; 3 g Dietary Fiber

Paré Pointer
When historians get together, all they talk about is old times.

Fast Cacciatore

Lots of saucy chicken. Serve over hot noodles.

Water	1 tbsp.	15 mL
Cornstarch	1 tbsp.	15 mL
Cooking oil	2 tsp.	10 mL
Boneless, skinless chicken breast halves (about 3), cut into thin strips	¾ lb.	340 g
Cooking oil	1 tsp.	5 mL
Sliced fresh mushrooms	2 cups	500 mL
Chopped onion	¼ cup	60 mL
Grated carrot	2 tbsp.	30 mL
Canned diced tomatoes	14 oz.	398 mL
Tomato sauce	7½ oz.	213 mL
Parsley flakes	1 tsp.	5 mL
Bay leaf	1	1
Granulated sugar	1 tsp.	5 mL
Garlic powder	⅛ tsp.	0.5 mL
Salt	½ tsp.	2 mL
Pepper	⅛ tsp.	0.5 mL
White (or alcohol-free white) wine	¼ cup	60 mL

Stir water into cornstarch in small cup. Set aside.

Heat wok or frying pan on medium-high. Add first amount of cooking oil. Add chicken strips. Stir-fry until no pink remains in chicken. Transfer to bowl.

Add second amount of cooking oil to hot wok. Add mushrooms, onion and carrot. Stir-fry for 3 to 5 minutes until tender-crisp. Add to chicken.

Add next 8 ingredients to hot wok. Stir until boiling. Reduce heat. Simmer, uncovered, for 10 minutes. Discard bay leaf. Stir cornstarch mixture. Stir into tomato mixture until boiling and thickened. Add chicken and vegetables. Heat through.

Stir in wine. Serves 4.

1 serving: 184 Calories; 5 g Total Fat; 587 mg Sodium; 21 g Protein; 11 g Carbohydrate; 2 g Dietary Fiber

 Create a quick next-day soup using leftover stir-fry–just add broth. Or make a salad, using pasta or salad greens and tossing with your favorite dressing.

Chicken

Chicken With Walnuts

Looks attractive with different shapes and brown sauce.
Walnuts add greatly to the flavor and texture.

Water	½ cup	125 mL
Cornstarch	1 tbsp.	15 mL
Low-sodium soy sauce	4 tsp.	20 mL
Sherry (or alcohol-free sherry)	1 tbsp.	15 mL
Brown sugar, packed	2 tsp.	10 mL
Salt	¼ tsp.	1 mL
Seasoned salt	¼ tsp.	1 mL
Pepper	⅛ tsp.	0.5 mL
Chicken bouillon powder	1 tsp.	5 mL
Garlic powder	¼ tsp.	1 mL
Peanut (or cooking) oil	1 tbsp.	15 mL
Boneless, skinless chicken breast halves (about 3), cut into thin strips	¾ lb.	340 g
Peanut (or cooking) oil	1 tsp.	5 mL
Medium onion, thinly sliced	1	1
Sliced celery	⅔ cup	150 mL
Sliced fresh mushrooms	1 cup	250 mL
Walnut pieces	¾ cup	175 mL
Coarsely chopped bok choy	3 cups	750 mL
Canned bamboo shoots, drained	8 oz.	227 mL
Canned sliced water chestnuts, drained	8 oz.	227 mL

Stir water into cornstarch in small bowl. Add next 8 ingredients. Stir. Set aside.

Heat wok or frying pan on medium-high. Add first amount of peanut oil. Add chicken strips. Stir-fry until no pink remains in chicken. Transfer to bowl.

Add second amount of peanut oil to hot wok. Add onion, celery and mushrooms. Stir-fry until slightly soft. Add chicken.

Add remaining 4 ingredients. Stir to heat through. Stir cornstarch mixture. Stir into chicken mixture until boiling and thickened. Makes 7 cups (1.75 L). Serves 6.

1 serving: 224 Calories; 11.8 g Total Fat; 499 mg Sodium; 17 g Protein; 13 g Carbohydrate; 2 g Dietary Fiber

Chicken 'N' Stuffing

Attractive contrasts of colors and shapes. Veggies keep their crunch.

Fine dry bread crumbs	1¼ cups	300 mL
Parsley flakes	1 tsp.	5 mL
Poultry seasoning	¾ tsp.	4 mL
Salt	¼ tsp.	1 mL
Pepper	1/16 tsp.	0.5 mL
Water	½ cup	125 mL
Cooking oil	1 tbsp.	15 mL
Boneless, skinless chicken breast halves (about 3), cut bite size	¾ lb.	340 g
Cooking oil	1 tsp.	5 mL
Chopped onion	⅓ cup	75 mL
Chopped celery	2 tbsp.	30 mL
Sliced or slivered zucchini, with peel	1 cup	250 mL
Frozen peas and carrots, partially thawed	1 cup	250 mL

Measure first 6 ingredients into small bowl. Stir. Reserve ¼ cup (60 mL). Set aside.

Heat wok or frying pan on medium-high. Add first amount of cooking oil. Add chicken. Stir-fry for about 4 minutes until no pink remains. Transfer to bowl.

Add second amount of cooking oil to hot wok. Add onion, celery, zucchini, peas and carrots. Stir-fry for about 2 minutes. Add chicken mixture. Stir to heat through. Add larger amount of bread crumb mixture. Stir until hot. Sprinkle with reserved crumb mixture. Makes 4 cups (1 L). Serves 4.

1 serving: 307 Calories; 7.6 g Total Fat; 524 mg Sodium; 26 g Protein; 33 g Carbohydrate; 3 g Dietary Fiber

Pictured on page 125.

 Partially freezing chicken before removing skin will make the job much easier.

Chicken Tetrazzini

Chicken with sauced pasta makes for a pleasant meal.

Bow pasta (about 3½ cups, 875 mL)	8 oz.	225 g
Boiling water	3 qts.	3 L
Cooking oil (optional)	1 tbsp.	15 mL
Salt	2 tsp.	10 mL
Condensed chicken broth	10 oz.	284 mL
Skim evaporated milk	⅓ cup	75 mL
Salt	¼ tsp.	1 mL
Pepper	⅛ tsp.	0.5 mL
Water	2 tbsp.	30 mL
Cornstarch	2 tbsp.	30 mL
Cooking oil	1 tbsp.	15 mL
Boneless, skinless chicken breast halves (about 3), cut bite size	¾ lb.	340 g
Chopped onion	1 cup	250 mL
Sliced fresh mushrooms	2 cups	500 mL
Sherry (or alcohol-free sherry)	2 tbsp.	30 mL
Grated Parmesan cheese	¼ cup	60 mL

Cook pasta in boiling water and first amounts of cooking oil and salt in large uncovered pot or Dutch oven for 12 to 14 minutes until tender but firm. Drain. Return pasta to pot. Cover to keep warm.

Mix chicken broth, evaporated milk, second amount of salt and pepper in medium bowl.

Stir water into cornstarch in small cup. Stir into chicken broth mixture. Set aside.

Heat wok or frying pan on medium-high. Add second amount of cooking oil. Add chicken strips and onion. Stir-fry for about 5 minutes until no pink remains in chicken and onion is soft.

Add mushrooms. Stir-fry until moisture is evaporated. Stir cornstarch mixture. Stir into chicken mixture until boiling and thickened.

Stir in sherry. Spread pasta on platter or 4 individual plates. Spoon chicken mixture over top. Sprinkle with Parmesan cheese. Makes 4 cups (1 L). Serves 4.

1 serving: 450 Calories; 8.5 g Total Fat; 854 mg Sodium; 36 g Protein; 55 g Carbohydrate; 3 g Dietary Fiber

Chicken

Chicken And Ham

A good blend of flavors. Goes well with hot mashed potatoes.

Water	¼ cup	60 mL
Cornstarch	2 tsp.	10 mL
Skim evaporated milk	¼ cup	60 mL
Chicken bouillon powder	1 tsp.	5 mL
Salt	¼ tsp.	1 mL
Pepper	¼ tsp.	1 mL
Cooking oil	1 tbsp.	15 mL
Boneless, skinless chicken breast halves (about 4), cut into strips	1 lb.	454 g
Chopped onion	¼ cup	60 mL
Chopped celery	2 tbsp.	30 mL
Ham cubes, about ¾ inch, 2 cm	1 cup	250 mL

Stir water into cornstarch in small bowl. Add next 4 ingredients. Stir. Set aside.

Heat wok or frying pan on medium-high. Add cooking oil. Add chicken strips, onion and celery. Stir-fry for 5 to 6 minutes until no pink remains in chicken.

Add ham. Stir-fry for 1 minute. Stir cornstarch mixture. Stir into chicken mixture until boiling and thickened. Makes 4 cups (1 L). Serves 4.

1 serving: 250 Calories; 9 g Total Fat; 927 mg Sodium; 34 g Protein; 6 g Carbohydrate; trace Dietary Fiber

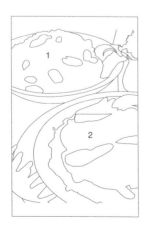

1. Tuna, Leek And Rice, page 64
2. Autumn Stir-Fry, page 10

Props Courtesy Of: Eaton's
Stokes
The Bay

Chicken Penne

Very quick to prepare. Not much chopping or cutting.

Penne pasta (about 6 oz., 170 g)	2 cups	500 mL
Boiling water	3 qts.	3 L
Cooking oil (optional)	1 tbsp.	15 mL
Salt	1 tbsp.	15 mL
Cooking oil	1 tbsp.	15 mL
Boneless, skinless chicken breast halves (about 3), cut bite size	¾ lb.	340 g
Yellow pepper strips	½ cup	125 mL
Peanuts (or cashews)	¼ cup	60 mL
Oyster sauce	⅓ cup	75 mL

Cook pasta in boiling water, first amount of cooking oil and salt in large uncovered pot or Dutch oven for 9 to 11 minutes until tender but firm. Drain. Return pasta to pot. Cover to keep warm.

Heat wok or frying pan on medium-high. Add second amount of cooking oil. Add chicken. Stir-fry for about 4 minutes until no pink remains in chicken.

Add yellow pepper strips and peanuts. Stir-fry for about 1 minute. Add pasta. Stir to heat through.

Add oyster sauce. Stir to coat well and heat through. Makes 6 cups (1.5 L). Serves 4.

1 serving: 381 Calories; 10.3 g Total Fat; 2043 mg Sodium; 28 g Protein; 43 g Carbohydrate; 2 g Dietary Fiber

Pictured on page 54 and back cover.

1. Apple Crumb Fry, page 56
2. Chicken Penne, above
3. Ginger Pork And Peppers, page 95
4. Hot Lettuce Salad, page 101

Props Courtesy Of: Clays Handmade Ceramic Tile & Stone
Dansk Gifts
Eaton's
The Bay

Chicken

Caramel Fruit

A rich, fresh fruit taste sensation. Spoon over
cake or ice cream to serve more people, or just enjoy as is.

Hard margarine (or butter)	1 tbsp.	15 mL
Brown sugar, packed	⅓ cup	75 mL
Water	1½ tbsp.	25 mL
Sliced banana, peaches, pears, strawberries or cherries	3 cups	750 mL
Icing (confectioner's) sugar	½ cup	125 mL
Ground cinnamon, sprinkle		

Combine margarine, brown sugar and water in wok or frying pan. Heat on medium-high, stirring continually, until mixture is bubbling.

Add fruit and icing sugar. Stir for about 2 minutes until fruit is hot and coated.

Sprinkle with cinnamon. Serves 4.

1 serving: 222 Calories; 3.3 g Total Fat; 41 mg Sodium; 1 g Protein; 50 g Carbohydrate; 3 g Dietary Fiber

Apple Crumb Fry

Top this tasty dessert with ice cream for a real treat. Goes together quickly.

Hard margarine (or butter)	1 tbsp.	15 mL
Water	3 tbsp.	50 mL
Granulated sugar	½ cup	125 mL
Medium cooking apples (McIntosh is good), peeled and sliced	4	4
Coarsely crushed crisp oatmeal cookies	¼ cup	60 mL

Combine first 4 ingredients in wok or frying pan. Heat on medium-high, stirring continually, for about 10 minutes until sugar is dissolved and liquid is reduced and turned caramel colored.

Remove from heat. Quickly stir in crushed cookies. Serves 4.

1 serving: 223 Calories; 4.1 g Total Fat; 35 mg Sodium; 1 g Protein; 49 g Carbohydrate; 2 g Dietary Fiber

Pictured on page 54.

Desserts

Peach Crunch

Rich peach flavor with crunchy gingersnap topping.

Hard margarine (or butter)	2 tbsp.	30 mL
Brown sugar, packed	1/4 cup	60 mL
Fresh peaches, peeled and sliced (or 3 cups, 750 mL, frozen, thawed)	4	4
Lemon juice	1/2 tsp.	2 mL
Gingersnap cookie crumbs	2 tbsp.	30 mL

Melt margarine in hot wok or frying pan. Add brown sugar, peach slices and lemon juice. Stir gently for 2 to 3 minutes until peaches are tender.

Sprinkle with cookie crumbs. Stir just to mix. Serves 4.

1 serving: 153 Calories; 6.3 g Total Fat; 98 mg Sodium; 1 g Protein; 25 g Carbohydrate; 1 g Dietary Fiber

Variation: Use 2 x 14 oz. (2 x 398 mL) canned sliced peaches, drained. Makes 2 cups (500 mL). Reduce brown sugar to 1 tbsp. (15 mL).

Pear Topping

A delicate pear flavor. Serve over ice cream or shortcake.

Hard margarine (or butter)	1/4 cup	60 mL
Granulated sugar	1/3 cup	75 mL
Ground allspice	1/2 tsp.	2 mL
Reserved pear juice	1/2 cup	125 mL
Canned sliced pears, drained and juice reserved	2 x 14 oz.	2 x 398 mL
Sliced almonds, toasted	2 tbsp.	30 mL

Melt margarine in hot wok or frying pan. Add sugar, allspice and reserved pear juice. Stir until sugar is dissolved.

Add pears and almonds. Stir gently for 1 minute. Makes 1 3/4 cups (425 mL). Serves 6.

1 serving: 210 Calories; 9.3 g Total Fat; 104 mg Sodium; 1 g Protein; 34 g Carbohydrate; 3 g Dietary Fiber

Mangoes

A delectable dish. Good with or without the almond flavoring.
So good with ice cream or a dollop of whipped topping.

Granulated sugar	½ cup	125 mL
Water	¼ cup	60 mL
Lemon juice	1 tsp.	5 mL
Mangoes, peeled and sliced	2	2
Almond flavoring (optional)	¼ tsp.	1 mL
Ground cinnamon, just a pinch		

Heat wok or frying pan on medium-high. Add sugar. Stir for about 3 minutes, until melted and dark tan in color.

Carefully add water as it will sputter a great deal. Stir for about 1 minute until blended.

Add lemon juice and mangoes. Stir gently for about 1 minute until soft and coated.

Stir in almond flavoring. Sprinkle with cinnamon. Serves 4.

1 serving: 169 Calories; 0.3 g Total Fat; 2 mg Sodium; 1 g Protein; 44 g Carbohydrate; 2 g Dietary Fiber

Pictured on page 17.

Raisin Crêpes

With crêpes made ahead, this fancy dessert can be created quickly.
Serve with your favorite vanilla or caramel sauce.

Hard margarine (or butter)	2 tsp.	10 mL
Water	3 tbsp.	50 mL
Part-skim ricotta cheese, mashed or sieved	1⅓ cups	325 mL
Rum flavoring	2 tsp.	10 mL
Ground cinnamon, just a pinch		
Ground nutmeg, just a pinch		
Coarsely chopped raisins	⅔ cup	150 mL
Prepared vanilla pudding in container (about 3½ oz., 99 g each)	2	2
Crêpes (6 inch, 15 cm, size)	8	8

(continued on next page)

Desserts

Melt margarine in hot wok or frying pan. Add water, ricotta cheese, rum flavoring, cinnamon and nutmeg. Stir. Add raisins. Stir until heated through.

Add pudding. Stir for about 1 minute until mixed. Makes 2 cups (500 mL) filling.

Divide down center of crêpes. Fold sides over center. Makes 8 crêpes.

1 filled crêpe: 152 Calories; 6 g Total Fat; 96 mg Sodium; 7 g Protein; 19 g Carbohydrate; 1 g Dietary Fiber

Banana Caramel

Rich, thick caramel-colored sauce to spoon warm over ice cream.

Hard margarine (or butter)	3 tbsp.	50 mL
Brown sugar, packed	¾ cup	175 mL
Dark corn syrup	2 tbsp.	30 mL
Vanilla	¼ tsp.	1 mL
Water (or apricot liqueur)	1 tbsp.	15 mL
Medium bananas, sliced	3	3

Melt margarine in hot wok or frying pan. Add brown sugar. Stir for about 2 minutes until light and frothy.

Add corn syrup and vanilla. Carefully add water as it will sputter a great deal. Stir for 1 minute.

Add banana. Stir for 1 minute to coat. Makes 2 cups (500 mL). Serves 4.

1 serving: 333 Calories; 9.1 g Total Fat; 124 mg Sodium; 1 g Protein; 66 g Carbohydrate; 1 g Dietary Fiber

Paré Pointer

Two friends—a gardener and a billiard player—mind their peas and cues.

Desserts

Orange Banana Medley

A bright and cheery dessert. Just the right amount of cinnamon.

Golden corn syrup	¼ cup	60 mL
Prepared orange juice	¼ cup	60 mL
Ground cinnamon	¹⁄₁₆ tsp.	0.5 mL
Canned mandarin orange segments, drained	10 oz.	284 mL
Medium bananas, sliced	2	2

Measure corn syrup, orange juice and cinnamon into wok or frying pan. Heat and stir on medium-high for about 2 minutes until bubbling.

Add orange segments and banana. Stir for about 1 minute until heated through. Makes 2 cups (500 mL). Serves 4.

1 serving: 129 Calories; 0.3 g Total Fat; 16 mg Sodium; 1 g Protein; 33 g Carbohydrate; 1 g Dietary Fiber

Chocolate Pears

Two flavors that are often combined—for delicious reasons!

Hard margarine (or butter)	1 tbsp.	15 mL
Golden corn syrup	2 tbsp.	30 mL
Granulated sugar	¼ cup	60 mL
Cocoa	2 tbsp.	30 mL
Water	2 tbsp.	30 mL
Vanilla	¼ tsp.	1 mL
Salt, just a pinch		
Fresh pears, peeled, seeded and cut into chunks (see Note)	3	3
Lemon juice, sprinkle		

Measure first 7 ingredients into wok or frying pan. Heat on medium-high and stir for about 1 minute until bubbling.

Sprinkle pears with lemon juice. Add to cocoa mixture. Stir gently for 1 minute until tender. Makes 2 cups (500 mL). Serves 4.

1 serving: 188 Calories; 3.7 g Total Fat; 42 mg Sodium; 1 g Protein; 42 g Carbohydrate; 5 g Dietary Fiber

Note: Canned pears, drained, may be used instead of fresh. Reduce sugar to 2 tbsp. (30 mL).

Very Berry Banana

Strawberries and bananas are always a winning combination.

Hard margarine (or butter)	2 tbsp.	30 mL
Granulated sugar	1/4 cup	60 mL
Lemon juice	2 tbsp.	30 mL
Bananas, sliced on diagonal	1²/₃ cups	400 mL
Mashed fresh strawberries	³/₄ cup	175 mL
Fresh strawberries, halved	18	18
Water	1/4 cup	60 mL
Cornstarch	1 tsp.	5 mL
Ground cinnamon	1/8 tsp.	0.5 mL
Almond flavoring	1/2 tsp.	2 mL
Chopped pecans (optional)	2 tbsp.	30 mL

Melt margarine in hot wok or frying pan. Stir in sugar. Stir for about 1 minute until mixture starts to bubble.

Sprinkle lemon juice over banana and strawberries in medium bowl. Stir to coat. Stir fruit gently into sugar mixture.

Stir water into cornstarch in small bowl. Add cinnamon, almond flavoring and pecans. Add to banana mixture. Stir until mixture starts to bubble. Stir for about 1 minute. Makes 3¹/₂ cups (875 mL). Serves 4.

1 serving: 183 Calories; 6.5 g Total Fat; 71 mg Sodium; 1 g Protein; 33 g Carbohydrate; 3 g Dietary Fiber

Pictured on page 17.

 tip   *For a low-fat alternative to cooking oil, try substituting broth or wine.*

Whitefish Amandine

Lots of color contrast. Toasted almonds give an added crunch.

Water	½ cup	125 mL
Cornstarch	1 tbsp.	15 mL
Lemon juice	1 tbsp.	15 mL
Parsley flakes	1 tsp.	5 mL
Granulated sugar	1 tsp.	5 mL
Salt	¾ tsp.	4 mL
Pepper, sprinkle		
Cooking oil	1 tsp.	5 mL
Sliced almonds	¼ cup	60 mL
Cooking oil	1 tbsp.	15 mL
Whitefish fillet, cut into ¾ inch (2 cm) cubes	¾ lb.	340 g
Fresh pea pods, halved crosswise (or 6 oz., 170 g, frozen, partially thawed)	2 cups	500 mL
Green, red and yellow pepper strips	1 cup	250 mL

Stir water into cornstarch in small bowl. Add next 5 ingredients. Stir. Set aside.

Heat wok or frying pan on medium. Add first amount of cooking oil. Add almonds. Stir-fry for about 30 seconds until lightly browned. Be careful not to scorch. Transfer to small plate.

Increase heat to medium-high. Add second amount of cooking oil to hot wok. Add fish and pea pods. Stir-fry for 4 to 5 minutes until fish is opaque. Transfer to bowl.

Add pepper strips to hot wok. Stir-fry for about 2 minutes until tender-crisp. Add fish and pea pods. Stir cornstarch mixture. Stir into fish mixture until boiling and thickened. Sprinkle with toasted almonds. Serves 4.

1 serving: 245 Calories; 13 g Total Fat; 557 mg Sodium; 20 g Protein; 13 g Carbohydrate; 3 g Dietary Fiber

 tip   *When choosing fish for stir-frying, pick varieties that have firm flesh: turbot, pike, monkfish, sea bass, shark, swordfish or tuna.*

Ocean Perch Stir-Fry

This stir-fry is as nice to look at as it is to eat.

Reserved juice from tomatoes		
All-purpose flour	2 tbsp.	30 mL
Salt	¼ tsp.	1 mL
Pepper	¼ tsp.	1 mL
Granulated sugar	½ tsp.	2 mL
Ground ginger	¼ tsp.	1 mL
Canned stewed tomatoes, drained and juice reserved	14 oz.	398 mL
Cooking oil	1 tsp.	5 mL
Small onion, thinly sliced	1	1
Sliced fresh mushrooms	1½ cups	375 mL
Sweet pickle relish	2 tsp.	10 mL
Worcestershire sauce	2 tsp.	10 mL
Cooking oil	1 tbsp.	15 mL
Ocean perch fillet, cut into 1 inch (2.5 cm) cubes	¾ lb.	340 g
Green onions, sliced	3	3

Gradually stir reserved juice from tomatoes into flour in medium bowl until smooth. Add next 5 ingredients. Stir. Set aside.

Heat wok or frying pan on medium-high. Add first amount of cooking oil. Add onion. Stir-fry for about 1 minute until soft.

Add mushrooms, relish and Worcestershire sauce. Stir-fry for about 2 minutes until golden. Transfer to bowl.

Add second amount of cooking oil to hot wok. Add fish and green onion. Stir-fry for about 3 minutes until fish is opaque. Add mushroom mixture. Stir flour mixture. Stir into fish mixture until boiling and thickened. Serves 4.

1 serving: 181 Calories; 5.8 g Total Fat; 538 mg Sodium; 19 g Protein; 14 g Carbohydrate; 2 g Dietary Fiber

---

Paré Pointer

When ghosts go for a ride, they fasten their sheet belts.

Tuna, Leek And Rice

A good dish with a mild fish flavor.

White wine (or apple juice)	¼ cup	60 mL
Hard margarine (or butter)	¼ cup	60 mL
Ground rosemary	1 tsp.	5 mL
Salt	½ tsp.	2 mL
Pepper	⅛ tsp.	0.5 mL
Cooking oil	1 tbsp.	15 mL
Tuna fillet, cut into short thin fingers	¾ lb.	340 g
Slivered or chopped leeks (white part only)	1 cup	250 mL
Dark romaine lettuce leaves, sliced and packed	1 cup	250 mL
Instant rice	1½ cups	375 mL
Boiling water	1½ cups	375 mL

Measure first 5 ingredients into small bowl. Stir. Set aside.

Heat wok or frying pan on medium-high. Add cooking oil. Add fish and leeks. Stir-fry for about 2 minutes until fish is opaque.

Add lettuce, rice and boiling water. Cover. Simmer until water is absorbed. Add wine mixture. Stir until heated through. Serves 4.

1 serving: 402 Calories; 16.9 g Total Fat; 525 mg Sodium; 22 g Protein; 36 g Carbohydrate; 1 g Dietary Fiber

Pictured on page 53.

Island Fish Stir-Fry

Coconut milk glazes this fish.

Canned coconut milk	½ cup	125 mL
All-purpose flour	1½ tbsp.	25 mL
White wine (or apple juice)	1 tbsp.	15 mL
Cooking oil	1 tbsp.	15 mL
Mahi mahi fillet (or other firm white fish), cut into ¾ inch (2 cm) cubes	¾ lb.	340 g
Salt, sprinkle		
Pepper, sprinkle		
Chopped macadamia nuts (or almonds), toasted	1 tbsp.	15 mL

(continued on next page)

Fish & Seafood

Gradually stir coconut milk into flour in small bowl until smooth. Add wine. Stir. Set aside.

Heat wok or frying pan on medium-high. Add cooking oil. Add fish. Stir-fry until fish is opaque. Sprinkle with salt and pepper. Transfer to medium bowl. Stir flour mixture. Add to wok. Stir until boiling and thickened. Add fish. Stir gently to heat through.

Sprinkle with nuts. Serves 4.

1 serving: 203 Calories; 12.9 g Total Fat; 80 mg Sodium; 17 g Protein; 5 g Carbohydrate; 1 g Dietary Fiber

Boston Bluefish Stir-Fry

Serve over hot noodles or in puff pastry shells for a special dish.

Vermouth	¼ cup	60 mL
Cornstarch	2 tsp.	10 mL
Lemon juice	1 tbsp.	15 mL
Salt	½ tsp.	2 mL
Pepper	¼ tsp.	1 mL
Ground mace	⅛ tsp.	0.5 mL
Ground thyme	⅛ tsp.	0.5 mL
Hard margarine (butter browns too fast)	1 tbsp.	15 mL
Leek (white part only), halved lengthwise and sliced	1	1
Sliced fresh mushrooms	2 cups	500 mL
Cooking oil	1 tbsp.	15 mL
Boston bluefish fillet, cut into ¾ inch (2 cm) cubes	1 lb.	454 g

Stir vermouth into cornstarch in small bowl. Add next 5 ingredients. Stir. Set aside.

Heat wok or frying pan on medium-high. Add margarine. Add leeks. Stir-fry for about 2 minutes until soft.

Add mushrooms. Stir-fry until soft. Transfer vegetables to bowl.

Add cooking oil and fish to hot wok. Stir-fry for about 2 minutes until fish is opaque. Stir cornstarch mixture. Stir gently into fish mixture until boiling and thickened. Add leek mixture. Stir gently to heat through. Serves 4.

1 serving: 243 Calories; 11.5 g Total Fat; 450 mg Sodium; 24 g Protein; 8 g Carbohydrate; 1 g Dietary Fiber

Fish & Seafood

Tuna-Sauced Noodles

Colorful presentation. Nice and creamy.

Canned tuna, with liquid	6½ oz.	184 g
Chopped pecans	3 tbsp.	50 mL
Hard margarine (or butter)	2 tbsp.	30 mL
Lemon juice	1½ tbsp.	25 mL
Dried sweet basil	½ tsp.	2 mL
Low-sodium soy sauce	½ tsp.	2 mL
Broad noodles	8 oz.	225 g
Boiling water	3 qts.	3 L
Cooking oil (optional)	1 tbsp.	15 mL
Salt	2 tsp.	10 mL
Cooking oil	2 tbsp.	30 mL
Frozen pea pods, partially thawed (or 2 cups, 500 mL, fresh)	6 oz.	170 g
Assorted colored pepper slivers	1 cup	250 mL
Chopped fresh parsley	2 tbsp.	30 mL
Sliced fresh mushrooms	1 cup	250 mL
Salt, sprinkle		
Pepper, sprinkle		

Measure first 6 ingredients into blender. Process until smooth. Set aside.

Cook noodles in boiling water, first amount of cooking oil and salt in large uncovered pot or Dutch oven for 5 to 7 minutes until tender but firm. Drain. Return noodles to pot. Cover to keep warm.

Heat wok or frying pan on medium-high. Add second amount of cooking oil. Add pea pods, pepper slivers, parsley and mushrooms. Sprinkle with salt and pepper. Stir-fry for 2 to 3 minutes until tender-crisp. Add tuna mixture. Stir until hot. Serve over hot noodles. Makes 8 cups (2 L). Serves 4.

1 serving: 443 Calories; 17.9 g Total Fat; 235 mg Sodium; 21 g Protein; 50 g Carbohydrate; 4 g Dietary Fiber

Variation: Omit pea pods. Add 2 cups (500 mL) frozen peas.

Paré Pointer

When his pet didn't come when called, he exclaimed, "Doggone."

Fish & Seafood

Dilled Snapper Fry

With asparagus and more. Excellent.

Low-fat plain yogurt	½ cup	125 mL
Lemon juice	½ tsp.	2 mL
Granulated sugar	½ tsp.	2 mL
Onion powder	¼ tsp.	1 mL
Dill weed (or 2 tsp., 10 mL, fresh, chopped)	½ tsp.	2 mL
Cooking oil	2 tsp.	10 mL
Fresh asparagus, cut into 1 inch (2.5 cm) lengths, tough ends discarded	½ lb.	225 g
Frozen pea pods, partially thawed (or 2 cups, 500 mL, fresh)	6 oz.	170 g
Frozen kernel corn	1 cup	250 mL
Cooking oil	1 tsp.	5 mL
Small onion, sliced	1	1
Cooking oil	1 tbsp.	15 mL
Snapper fillet, cut into ¾ inch (2 cm) pieces	¾ lb.	340 g
Chopped chives	1 tbsp.	15 mL
Salt, sprinkle		
Pepper, sprinkle		

Measure first 5 ingredients into small bowl. Stir. Set aside.

Heat wok or frying pan on medium-high. Add first amount of cooking oil. Add asparagus, pea pods and frozen corn. Stir-fry for 4 to 5 minutes. Transfer to bowl.

Add second amount of cooking oil to hot wok. Add onion. Stir-fry for about 2 minutes until soft. Add to vegetables in bowl.

Add third amount of cooking to hot wok. Add fish and chives. Stir-fry for about 4 minutes until fish is opaque. Sprinkle with salt and pepper. Add vegetable mixture. Stir-fry until heated through. Add yogurt mixture. Stir until bubbling. Makes 4 cups (1 L). Serves 4.

1 serving: 243 Calories; 9.1 g Total Fat; 82 mg Sodium; 24 g Protein; 19 g Carbohydrate; 3 g Dietary Fiber

Pictured on page 90.

Speedy Shrimp

A quick rice dish all doctored up.

Cooking oil	2 tsp.	10 mL
Frozen Oriental vegetable mix	1 lb.	454 g
Frozen cooked small shrimp, thawed under cold running water	½ lb.	225 g
Instant rice	1½ cups	375 mL
Chicken bouillon powder	1 tsp.	5 mL
Salt	¾ tsp.	4 mL
Pepper	¼ tsp.	1 mL
Boiling water	1½ cups	375 mL

Heat wok or frying pan on medium-high. Add cooking oil. Run cold water over vegetable mix to partially thaw. Cut large pieces into uniform size. Add vegetable mix to wok. Stir-fry for 4 to 5 minutes.

Add shrimp. Stir-fry for about 1 minute until hot.

Add remaining 5 ingredients. Stir. Reduce heat. Cover. Steam for 1 minute. Remove from heat. Let stand for 6 minutes until all moisture is absorbed. Serves 4.

1 serving: 269 Calories; 3.8 g Total Fat; 860 mg Sodium; 16 g Protein; 42 g Carbohydrate; 3 g Dietary Fiber

Sweet And Sour Shrimp

This is traditionally served over hot rice.

Water	2 tbsp.	30 mL
Cornstarch	1 tbsp.	15 mL
White vinegar	2 tbsp.	30 mL
Granulated sugar	2 tbsp.	30 mL
Low-sodium soy sauce	1 tbsp.	15 mL
Ketchup	1 tbsp.	15 mL
Salt	½ tsp.	2 mL
Paprika	⅛ tsp.	0.5 mL
Cooking oil	1½ tsp.	7 mL
Large green pepper, diced	1	1
Cooking oil	1½ tsp.	7 mL
Fresh raw small shrimp, peeled and deveined	¾ lb.	340 g

(continued on next page)

Stir water into cornstarch in small bowl. Add next 6 ingredients. Stir. Set aside.

Heat wok or frying pan on medium-high. Add first amount of cooking oil. Add green pepper. Stir-fry for 1 minute. Transfer with slotted spoon to bowl.

Add second amount of cooking oil to hot wok. Add shrimp. Stir-fry until pinkish and curled. Add green pepper. Stir cornstarch mixture. Stir into shrimp mixture until boiling and thickened. Serves 4.

1 serving: 164 Calories; 4.8 g Total Fat; 674 mg Sodium; 18 g Protein; 12 g Carbohydrate; trace Dietary Fiber

---

Blackened Shrimp

Blackened in taste, not in color. There is a nip to
this pop-in-your mouth appetizer. Serve with cocktail picks.

Fresh raw medium shrimp, peeled and deveined, patted dry with paper towel	1 lb.	454 g
Cooking oil	2 tsp.	10 mL
Salt	1/2 tsp.	2 mL
Pepper	1/4 tsp.	1 mL
Garlic powder	1/4 tsp.	1 mL
Onion powder	1/4 tsp.	1 mL
Celery salt	1/4 tsp.	1 mL
Dry mustard	1/4 tsp.	1 mL
Cayenne pepper	1/4 tsp.	1 mL
Chili powder	1/4 tsp.	1 mL

Toss shrimp with cooking oil in medium bowl.

Mix remaining 8 ingredients in small bowl. Heat wok or frying pan on medium-high. Add shrimp to wok. Sprinkle with spice mixture. Stir-fry until sizzling. Wok bottom will blacken rather than shrimp. Makes 36.

3 shrimp: 48 Calories; 1.5 g Total Fat; 199 mg Sodium; 8 g Protein; 1 g Carbohydrate; trace Dietary Fiber

Pictured on front cover.

Garlic Shrimp

A nice garlic butter flavor that doesn't overpower the shrimp taste.
Makes a great appetizer, warm or cold.

Olive (or cooking) oil	3 tbsp.	50 mL
Butter (or hard margarine), melted (butter is best)	3 tbsp.	50 mL
Garlic cloves, minced	2	2
Lemon juice	1 tbsp.	15 mL
Chopped fresh parsley	2 tbsp.	30 mL
Onion powder	¼ tsp.	1 mL
Fresh raw large shrimp, tails intact, peeled and deveined	¾ lb.	340 g

Salt, light sprinkle
Pepper, sprinkle

Measure first 6 ingredients into medium bowl. Stir well.

Add shrimp. Stir well to coat. Cover. Marinate in refrigerator for 30 minutes, stirring once or twice.

Heat wok or frying pan on medium-high. Remove shrimp with slotted spoon to wok. Discard marinade. Stir-fry shrimp for about 5 minutes until pinkish and curled. Sprinkle with salt and pepper. Makes about 24.

3 shrimp: 131 Calories; 10.3 g Total Fat; 108 mg Sodium; 9 g Protein; 1 g Carbohydrate; trace Dietary Fiber

1. Far East Beef, page 24
2. Oriental Beef, page 14
3. Spring Rolls, page 141

Props Courtesy Of: Chintz & Company
Salisbury Greenhouses

Fish & Seafood

Crab And Artichokes

May be served on toasted baguette slices or with hot noodles or rice.

Milk	¹/₂ cup	125 mL
Cornstarch	2 tsp.	10 mL
Salt	¹/₄ tsp.	1 mL
Pepper	¹/₁₆ tsp.	0.5 mL
Garlic salt	¹/₁₆ tsp.	0.5 mL
Chicken bouillon powder	1 tsp.	5 mL
Cooking oil	1 tbsp.	15 mL
Chopped onion	¹/₂ cup	125 mL
Chopped fresh mushrooms	1 cup	250 mL
Crabmeat, cartilage removed (or imitation crabmeat)	³/₄ lb.	340 g
Canned artichokes, drained and cut up	14 oz.	398 mL
Sherry (or alcohol-free sherry)	1¹/₂ tbsp.	25 mL
Grated medium Cheddar cheese	¹/₄ cup	60 mL

Stir milk into cornstarch in small bowl. Add next 4 ingredients. Stir. Set aside.

Heat wok or frying pan on medium-high. Add cooking oil. Add onion and mushrooms. Stir-fry until soft.

Add crabmeat and artichoke. Stir cornstarch mixture. Stir into crab mixture until boiling and thickened.

Stir in sherry and cheese. Makes 2¹/₂ cups (625 mL).

¹/₂ cup (125 mL): 162 Calories; 6.1 g Total Fat; 841 mg Sodium; 17 g Protein; 9 g Carbohydrate; 3 g Dietary Fiber

1. Pork And Olives, page 86
2. Mediterranean Beef, page 27

Props Courtesy Of: Le Gnome
The Bay

Scallop Citrus Fry

You will love the aroma while stir-frying this.

Low-sodium soy sauce	2 tbsp.	30 mL
Cornstarch	2 tsp.	10 mL
Grapefruit juice	2 tbsp.	30 mL
Prepared orange juice	2 tbsp.	30 mL
Lemon juice	1 tsp.	5 mL
Ground ginger	1/4 tsp.	1 mL
Cooking oil	1 tbsp.	15 mL
Scallops, halved	3/4 lb.	340 g
Green onions, sliced into 1 inch (2.5 cm) lengths	4	4
Small pink grapefruit, peeled and sectioned or sliced	1/2	1/2
Medium orange, peeled and sectioned (use more orange than grapefruit)	1	1

Stir soy sauce into cornstarch in small bowl. Add next 4 ingredients. Stir. Set aside.

Heat wok or frying pan on medium-high. Add cooking oil. Add scallops and green onion. Stir-fry for 4 to 5 minutes until scallops are white and opaque.

Add grapefruit and orange sections. Stir cornstarch mixture. Stir into scallop mixture until boiling and thickened. Serves 4.

1 serving: 151 Calories; 4.2 g Total Fat; 451 mg Sodium; 16 g Protein; 13 g Carbohydrate; 1 g Dietary Fiber

Saucy Scallops

Nice combination of ingredients that doesn't overpower the delicate scallop flavor.

Salad dressing (or mayonnaise)	1/3 cup	75 mL
Dark greens (romaine lettuce or spinach), chopped and packed	1/4 cup	60 mL
Chopped green onion	1/4 cup	60 mL
Milk	2 tbsp.	30 mL
Dill weed	1/2 tsp.	2 mL
Cooking oil	1 tbsp.	15 mL
Scallops, cut up if large	3/4 lb.	340 g
Fresh pea pods (or 6 oz., 170 g, frozen, partially thawed)	2 cups	500 mL

(continued on next page)

74

Fish & Seafood

Mix first 5 ingredients in small bowl. Set aside.

Heat wok or frying pan on medium-high. Add cooking oil. Add scallops and pea pods. Stir-fry for 4 to 5 minutes until scallops are white and opaque. Add dressing mixture to scallop mixture. Stir for 30 seconds to heat through. Serves 4.

1 serving: 237 Calories; 14.4 g Total Fat; 273 mg Sodium; 16 g Protein; 10 g Carbohydrate; 2 g Dietary Fiber

Shrimp Creole

This eye-appealing dish is mildly spiced. To save time, use frozen mixed pepper strips if your grocery store carries them. Serve on a bed of hot rice.

Canned diced tomatoes, drained	14 oz.	398 mL
Ketchup	1 tbsp.	15 mL
Chili powder	1 tsp.	5 mL
Brown sugar, packed	2 tsp.	10 mL
Salt	1 tsp.	5 mL
Cayenne pepper	1/8 tsp.	0.5 mL
Cooking oil	2 tsp.	10 mL
Small green pepper, cut into strips	1/2	1/2
Small red pepper, cut into strips	1/2	1/2
Small yellow pepper, cut into strips	1/2	1/2
Thinly sliced celery	1/3 cup	75 mL
Sliced onion	1/2 cup	125 mL
Frozen cooked medium shrimp, thawed under cold running water	1 lb.	454 g

Measure first 6 ingredients into small bowl. Stir. Set aside.

Heat wok or frying pan on medium-high. Add cooking oil. Add pepper strips, celery and onion. Stir-fry for about 3 minutes.

Add shrimp. Stir-fry until hot and sizzling. Add tomato mixture. Stir to heat through. Makes about 3 cups (750 mL). Serves 4.

1 serving: 186 Calories; 4 g Total Fat; 1166 mg Sodium; 25 g Protein; 12 g Carbohydrate; 2 g Dietary Fiber

Pictured on page 90.

Asparagus And Shrimp

A showy dish with a nice blend of flavors. Serve over
hot white rice for color contrast.

Cooking oil	1 tbsp.	15 mL
Medium onion, sliced	1	1
Fresh asparagus, cut into 2 inch (5 cm) lengths, tough ends discarded	1 lb.	454 g
Salt, sprinkle		
Pepper, sprinkle		
Cooking oil	1 tsp.	5 mL
Fresh raw medium shrimp, peeled and deveined	¾ lb.	340 g
Low-sodium soy sauce	1 tbsp.	15 mL
Sesame seeds, toasted	1 tbsp.	15 mL

Heat wok or frying pan on medium-high. Add first amount of cooking oil. Add onion and asparagus. Stir-fry for 5 to 6 minutes until tender-crisp. Sprinkle with salt and pepper. Transfer to bowl.

Add second amount of cooking oil to hot wok. Add shrimp. Stir-fry for 4 to 5 minutes until pinkish and curled. Add vegetables. Stir to heat through.

Add soy sauce. Stir.

Sprinkle with sesame seeds. Serves 4.

1 serving: 224 Calories; 12.1 g Total Fat; 286 mg Sodium; 22 g Protein; 8 g Carbohydrate; 3 g Dietary Fiber

 Seat your guests at the table just before adding shrimp to a stir-fry. Have them pass the buns, serve the salad, or whatever. This way, the stir-fry can be served immediately. There is nothing more succulent than a fresh cooked shrimp. There is nothing more unappetizing than a dry, tough shrimp that has been overcooked or left to sit too long.

Shrimp And Artichokes

*Serve over hot noodles or penne pasta. This is
a must for your next dinner party.*

Milk	½ cup	125 mL
Cornstarch	1 tbsp.	15 mL
Sherry (or alcohol-free sherry)	1 tbsp.	15 mL
Worcestershire sauce	1 tsp.	5 mL
Salt	¼ tsp.	1 mL
Pepper	¹⁄₁₆ tsp.	0.5 mL
Cooking oil	1 tbsp.	15 mL
Sliced fresh mushrooms	1 cup	250 mL
Canned artichoke hearts, drained and halved	14 oz.	398 mL
Cooking oil	1 tsp.	5 mL
Fresh raw medium shrimp, peeled and deveined	¾ lb.	340 g
Grated Parmesan cheese	2 tbsp.	30 mL

Stir milk into cornstarch in small bowl. Add next 4 ingredients. Stir. Set aside.

Heat wok or frying pan on medium-high. Add first amount of cooking oil. Add mushrooms and artichoke. Stir-fry for about 2 minutes until golden. Transfer to bowl.

Add second amount of cooking oil to hot wok. Add shrimp. Stir-fry until shrimp is pinkish and curled. Add mushroom mixture. Stir cornstarch mixture. Stir into shrimp mixture until boiling and thickened.

Sprinkle with Parmesan cheese. Serves 4.

1 serving: 201 Calories; 7.5 g Total Fat; 563 mg Sodium; 22 g Protein; 11 g Carbohydrate; 3 g Dietary Fiber

 tip   *In a hurry? Use either canned or frozen cooked shrimp and pre-cut ingredients such as canned sliced water chestnuts to speed up preparation time.*

Fish & Seafood

Crab And Veggies

Red pepper sauce adds to this blend of flavors.
Also try this with a firm-flesh fish.

RED PEPPER SAUCE

Small red pepper	1	1
Medium tomato, peeled and cut up	1	1
Red wine vinegar	1 tsp.	5 mL
Minced onion flakes	1 tsp.	5 mL
Garlic powder (or ½ clove, minced)	⅛ tsp.	0.5 mL
Granulated sugar	½ tsp.	2 mL
Dried sweet basil	⅛ tsp.	0.5 mL
Dried whole oregano	⅛ tsp.	0.5 mL
Cooking oil	1 tbsp.	15 mL
Small red onion, sliced	1	1
Sliced celery	1 cup	250 mL
Frozen cut green beans, partially thawed	1 cup	250 mL
Sliced fresh mushrooms	1 cup	250 mL
Cooking oil	1 tsp.	5 mL
Imitation crabmeat (or lobster), coarsely chopped	¾ lb.	340 g
Salt, sprinkle		
Pepper, sprinkle		

Red Pepper Sauce: Quarter red pepper. Remove seeds. Place on broiler pan, skin side up. Broil until charred black. Cool. Remove skin. Cut up pepper and place in blender.

Add next 7 ingredients to blender. Process until smooth. Makes ½ cup (125 mL) sauce.

Heat wok or frying pan on medium-high. Add first amount of cooking oil. Add red onion, celery and green beans. Stir-fry for about 4 minutes.

Add mushrooms. Stir-fry for about 2 minutes until soft. Transfer to bowl.

Add second amount of cooking oil to hot wok. Add crabmeat. Stir-fry until hot. Sprinkle with salt and pepper. Add vegetables. Stir to heat through. Add red pepper sauce. Stir until bubbling. Makes 5 cups (1.25 L). Serves 4.

1 serving: *176 Calories; 5.9 g Total Fat; 132 mg Sodium; 22 g Protein; 9 g Carbohydrate;*
2 g Dietary Fiber

Three Seafood Fry

Contains shrimp, tuna and crab. Serve over hot shell
pasta to keep the seafood theme.

Milk	½ cup	125 mL
Cornstarch	1 tbsp.	15 mL
Worcestershire sauce	1 tsp.	5 mL
Salt	¼ tsp.	1 mL
Cooking oil	1 tsp.	5 mL
Medium onion, thinly sliced	1	1
Small green pepper, chopped	1	1
Sliced fresh mushrooms	1 cup	250 mL
Cooking oil	1 tbsp.	15 mL
Fresh raw medium shrimp, peeled and deveined	¼ lb.	113 g
Tuna fillet, cut into ¾ inch (2 cm) cubes	¼ lb.	113 g
Crabmeat, cartilage removed (or imitation crabmeat)	¼ lb.	113 g
Sherry (or alcohol-free sherry)	1 tbsp.	15 mL

Stir milk into cornstarch in small bowl. Add next 2 ingredients. Stir. Set aside.

Heat wok or frying pan on medium-high. Add first amount of cooking oil. Add onion and green pepper. Stir-fry for 3 minutes.

Add mushrooms. Stir-fry for about 2 minutes until golden. Transfer to bowl.

Add second amount of cooking oil to hot wok. Add shrimp and tuna. Stir-fry for about 5 minutes until shrimp is pinkish and curled and tuna is opaque.

Add crabmeat and vegetables. Stir to heat through. Stir cornstarch mixture. Stir into seafood mixture until boiling and thickened. Stir in sherry. Serves 4.

1 serving: 170 Calories; 6.2 g Total Fat; 408 mg Sodium; 19 g Protein; 8 g Carbohydrate; 1 g Dietary Fiber

Pictured on page 90.

Salmon And Pea Pod Pasta

A mild sweet and sour flavor with a hint of ginger.

Penne pasta (about 8 oz., 225 g)	2⅔ cups	650 mL
Boiling water	3 qts.	3 L
Cooking oil (optional)	1 tbsp.	15 mL
Salt	2 tsp.	10 mL
Water	½ cup	125 mL
Cornstarch	1 tbsp.	15 mL
Rice vinegar	1 tbsp.	15 mL
Low-sodium soy sauce	1 tbsp.	15 mL
Granulated sugar	1 tbsp.	15 mL
Garlic powder	⅛ tsp.	0.5 mL
Finely grated gingerroot	1 tsp.	5 mL
Cooking oil	2 tsp.	10 mL
Frozen pea pods, partially thawed (or 2 cups, 500 mL, fresh)	6 oz.	170 g
Green onions, sliced	2-3	2-3
Cooking oil	2 tsp.	10 mL
Salmon fillet, cut into ¾ inch (2 cm) cubes	¾ lb.	340 g

Cook pasta in boiling water, first amount of cooking oil and salt in large uncovered pot or Dutch oven for 10 to 12 minutes until tender but firm. Drain. Return pasta to pot. Cover to keep warm.

Stir water into cornstarch in small bowl. Add next 5 ingredients. Stir. Stir into pasta in pot over medium until boiling and thickened.

Heat wok or frying pan on medium-high. Add second amount of cooking oil. Add pea pods and green onion. Stir-fry for 2 to 3 minutes. Add to pasta.

Add third amount of cooking oil to hot wok. Add salmon. Stir-fry for 4 to 5 minutes until salmon flakes when tested with fork. Add to pasta mixture. Toss gently to heat through. Serves 4.

1 serving: 445 Calories; 14.5 g Total Fat; 203 mg Sodium; 26 g Protein; 51 g Carbohydrate; 3 g Dietary Fiber

Cod Stir-Fry

A good choice for the next time you serve cod.

Plain yogurt	½ cup	125 mL
Lemon juice	1 tbsp.	15 mL
Grated lemon zest (no white pith)	½ tsp.	2 mL
Brown sugar, packed	1 tbsp.	15 mL
Cooking oil	1 tbsp.	15 mL
Small red onion, sliced	1	1
Medium red pepper, cut into matchsticks	1	1
Cooking oil	2 tsp.	10 mL
Zucchini, 5 inch (12.5 cm) length, with peel, cut into thin fingers	1	1
Sliced fresh mushrooms	2 cups	500 mL
Frozen pea pods, partially thawed (or 2 cups, 500 mL, fresh)	6 oz.	170 g
Cooking oil	1 tsp.	5 mL
Cod fillet, cut into fingers	¾ lb.	340 g
Salt, sprinkle		
Pepper, sprinkle		
Sliced pimiento-stuffed green olives	¼ cup	60 mL
Grated Parmesan cheese, sprinkle		

Stir first 4 ingredients in small bowl. Set aside.

Heat wok or frying pan on medium-high. Add first amount of cooking oil. Add red onion and red pepper. Stir-fry for about 2 minutes until soft. Transfer to bowl.

Add second amount of cooking oil to hot wok. Add zucchini, mushrooms and pea pods. Stir-fry for about 3 minutes. Add to vegetables in bowl.

Add third amount of cooking oil to hot wok. Add fish. Stir-fry for about 2 minutes until opaque. Sprinkle with salt and pepper. Add vegetables. Add yogurt mixture. Stir gently until heated through.

Add olives. Stir. Sprinkle with Parmesan cheese. Serves 4.

1 serving: 210 Calories; 8.4 g Total Fat; 123 mg Sodium; 19 g Protein; 15 g Carbohydrate; 3 g Dietary Fiber

Seafood Stir-Fry

*Good texture. A wee bite from the horseradish which adds
to the good taste. Serve over hot rice.*

Chili sauce	3 tbsp.	50 mL
Ketchup	1 tbsp.	15 mL
Prepared horseradish	2 tsp.	10 mL
Lemon juice	2 tsp.	10 mL
Worcestershire sauce	½ tsp.	2 mL
Onion powder	¼ tsp.	1 mL
Cooking oil	1 tbsp.	15 mL
Fresh raw medium shrimp, peeled and deveined	½ lb.	225 g
Crabmeat, cartilage removed (or imitation crabmeat)	¼ lb.	113 g
Chopped chives (or green onion)	¼ cup	60 mL
Salt, sprinkle		
Pepper, sprinkle		
Cayenne pepper, light sprinkle		

Stir first 6 ingredients in small bowl. Set aside.

Heat wok or frying pan on medium-high. Add cooking oil. Add shrimp.
Stir-fry for about 1 minute until shrimp is pinkish and curled.

Add crabmeat and chives. Stir-fry to heat through. Sprinkle with salt,
pepper and cayenne pepper. Add sauce. Stir until seafood is coated and
heated through. Serves 4.

*1 serving: 138 Calories; 4.8 g Total Fat; 470 mg Sodium; 17 g Protein; 6 g Carbohydrate;
1 g Dietary Fiber*

Variation: Total weight, ¾ lb. (340 g) of seafood can be made up of
shrimp, crab and scallops if desired.

 *To remove the smell of onion, garlic or fish from your hands, rinse
them under running water, rub with baking soda, then rinse again.*

Fish & Seafood

Nutty Pork And Onion

A great dish with a bit of a nip. Add more cayenne pepper if you like.

Water	⅓ cup	75 mL
Cornstarch	1 tbsp.	15 mL
White vinegar	1½ tbsp.	25 mL
Low-sodium soy sauce	1 tbsp.	15 mL
Brown sugar, packed	1 tbsp.	15 mL
Chicken bouillon powder	1 tsp.	5 mL
Onion powder	¼ tsp.	1 mL
Cayenne pepper	¼ tsp.	1 mL
Cooking oil	1 tbsp.	15 mL
Pork tenderloin, cut into thin strips	¾ lb.	340 g
Salt, sprinkle		
Pepper, sprinkle		
Cooking oil	1 tsp.	5 mL
Medium red onion, sliced	1	1
Garlic clove, minced (or ¼ tsp., 1 mL, powder)	1	1
Coarsely chopped peanuts	3 tbsp.	50 mL

Stir water into cornstarch in small bowl. Add next 6 ingredients. Stir. Set aside.

Heat wok or frying pan on medium-high. Add first amount of cooking oil. Add pork strips. Stir-fry until no pink remains in pork. Sprinkle with salt and pepper. Transfer to bowl.

Add second amount of cooking oil to hot wok. Add red onion and garlic. Stir-fry for 3 minutes. Add pork. Stir cornstarch mixture. Stir into pork mixture until boiling and thickened.

Stir in peanuts. Makes 2½ cups (625 mL). Serves 4.

1 serving: 216 Calories; 10.4 g Total Fat; 364 mg Sodium; 20 g Protein; 10 g Carbohydrate; 1 g Dietary Fiber

 tip *When mincing garlic, place the salt normally added to the recipe directly onto the garlic while it's still on the cutting board. The salt will absorb the juices and make it easier to slide the tiny pieces off the board.*

Noodles And Pork

Nice flavor and texture. Grated cheese melts and coats each serving.

Medium or broad noodles	8 oz.	225 g
Boiling water	3 qts.	3 L
Cooking oil (optional)	1 tbsp.	15 mL
Salt	2 tsp.	10 mL
Canned kernel corn, drained	12 oz.	341 mL
Chopped pimiento, drained	2 oz.	57 mL
Salt	¾ tsp.	4 mL
Pepper	¼ tsp.	1 mL
Hard margarine (or butter)	1 tbsp.	15 mL
Dry bread crumbs	¼ cup	60 mL
Cooking oil	1 tbsp.	15 mL
Boneless pork loin, cut into thin strips	¾ lb.	340 g
Sliced celery	½ cup	125 mL
Grated part-skim mozzarella cheese	1 cup	250 mL

Cook noodles in boiling water and first amounts of cooking oil and salt in large uncovered pot or Dutch oven for 5 to 7 minutes until tender but firm. Drain. Return noodles to pot. Cover to keep warm.

Stir corn, pimiento, second amount of salt and pepper in small bowl. Set aside.

Heat margarine and bread crumbs in cup in microwave to melt margarine. Stir. Set aside.

Heat wok or frying pan on medium-high. Add second amount of cooking oil. Add pork strips and celery. Stir-fry for about 5 minutes until no pink remains in pork. Stir in noodles and corn mixture. Stir-fry until bubbling hot. Sprinkle with bread crumbs and cheese. Makes 6 cups (1.5 L). Serves 4.

1 serving: 549 Calories; 17.8 g Total Fat; 976 mg Sodium; 36 g Protein; 61 g Carbohydrate; 3 g Dietary Fiber

Pork

Sweet And Sour Pork

Add hot pepper sauce gradually, tasting once or twice,
until desired "temperature."

Water	½ cup	125 mL
Cornstarch	1 tbsp.	15 mL
White vinegar	1 tbsp.	15 mL
Granulated sugar	1 tbsp.	15 mL
Low-sodium soy sauce	2 tbsp.	30 mL
Ground ginger	¼ tsp.	1 mL
Hot pepper sauce (more or less)	⅛ tsp.	0.5 mL
Garlic powder	¼ tsp.	1 mL
Cooking oil	1 tbsp.	15 mL
Boneless pork loin, cut into thin strips	¾ lb.	340 g
Salt, sprinkle		
Pepper, sprinkle		
Cooking oil	1 tsp.	5 mL
Broccoli florets	1 cup	250 mL
Cauliflower florets	1 cup	250 mL
Medium cooking apple (such as Granny Smith), peeled and thinly sliced	1	1
Green onions, cut into 1 inch (2.5 cm) lengths	3	3

Stir water into cornstarch in small bowl. Add next 6 ingredients. Stir. Set aside.

Heat wok or frying pan on medium-high. Add first amount of cooking oil. Add pork strips. Stir-fry until no pink remains in pork. Sprinkle with salt and pepper. Transfer to bowl.

Add second amount of cooking oil to hot wok. Add broccoli and cauliflower. Stir-fry for 4 to 5 minutes until tender-crisp. Add to pork in bowl.

Add apple and green onion to hot wok. Stir-fry until apple is tender-crisp. Add pork mixture. Stir cornstarch mixture. Stir into pork mixture until boiling and thickened. Serves 4.

1 serving: 224 Calories; 9.8 g Total Fat; 378 mg Sodium; 21 g Protein; 14 g Carbohydrate; 2 g Dietary Fiber

Pork

Veggie Pork

Serve this very tasty dish with hot potatoes, rice or pasta.

Water	½ cup	125 mL
Cornstarch	1 tbsp.	15 mL
Beef bouillon powder	1 tsp.	5 mL
Ground thyme	⅛ tsp.	0.5 mL
Dried sweet basil	⅛ tsp.	0.5 mL
Salt	⅛ tsp.	0.5 mL
Pepper	⅛ tsp.	0.5 mL
Cooking oil	1 tbsp.	15 mL
Lean boneless pork loin, sliced into ⅛ inch (3 mm) thin strips	¾ lb.	340 g
Frozen California mixed vegetables (including broccoli and cauliflower), thawed	4 cups	1 L

Stir water into cornstarch in small bowl. Add next 5 ingredients. Stir. Set aside.

Heat wok or frying pan on medium-high. Add cooking oil. Add pork strips. Stir-fry until no pink remains in pork. Transfer to bowl.

Add vegetables to hot wok. Stir-fry until tender-crisp. Add pork. Stir to heat through. Stir cornstarch mixture. Stir into pork mixture until boiling and thickened. Makes 4 cups (1 L). Serves 4.

1 serving: 247 Calories; 8.7 g Total Fat; 342 mg Sodium; 23 g Protein; 20 g Carbohydrate; 6 g Dietary Fiber

Pork And Olives

For olive lovers everywhere!

Long grain white rice	¾ cup	175 mL
Water	1½ cups	375 mL
Salt	¾ tsp.	4 mL
Cooking oil	1 tbsp.	15 mL
Boneless pork loin, cut into thin strips	¾ lb.	340 g
Canned diced tomatoes, drained	14 oz.	398 mL
Sliced pimiento-stuffed green olives	¼ cup	60 mL

(continued on next page)

Pork

Cook rice in water and salt in medium covered saucepan for 15 to 20 minutes until tender and moisture is absorbed. Cover to keep warm.

Heat wok or frying pan on medium-high. Add cooking oil. Add pork strips. Stir-fry for about 4 minutes until no pink remains.

Add tomatoes and olives. Stir to heat through. Spread rice on platter or 4 individual plates. Spoon pork mixture over top. Serves 4.

1 serving: 319 Calories; 9.6 g Total Fat; 831 mg Sodium; 22 g Protein; 35 g Carbohydrate; 2 g Dietary Fiber

Pictured on page 72.

Fruity Pork And Rice

A quick way to enjoy the ever-favorite combination of pork and apple.

Long grain white rice	¾ cup	175 mL
Water	1½ cups	375 mL
Salt	1 tsp.	5 mL
Pepper	¼ tsp.	1 mL
Cooking oil	1 tbsp.	15 mL
Boneless pork loin, cut into ¾ inch (2 cm) cubes	¾ lb.	340 g
Cooking oil	1 tsp.	5 mL
Sliced red onion	½ cup	125 mL
Sliced celery	½ cup	125 mL
Medium cooking apple (such as McIntosh), with peel, cubed	1	1

Cook rice in water, salt and pepper in medium covered saucepan for 15 to 20 minutes until tender and water is absorbed. Cover to keep warm.

Heat wok or frying pan on medium-high. Add first amount of cooking oil. Add pork cubes. Stir-fry for about 4 minutes until no pink remains. Transfer to bowl.

Add second amount of cooking oil to hot wok. Add red onion and celery. Stir-fry for 3 minutes.

Add apple. Stir-fry for 1 minute. Add pork. Stir to heat through. Spread rice on platter or 4 individual plates. Spoon pork mixture over top. Serves 4.

1 serving: 327 Calories; 9.9 g Total Fat; 748 mg Sodium; 22 g Protein; 37 g Carbohydrate; 2 g Dietary Fiber

Pictured on page 89.

Pork

Polynesian Pork

Complete this sweet and sour dish by serving over a bed of hot rice.

Low-sodium soy sauce	1 tbsp.	15 mL
Cornstarch	1 tbsp.	15 mL
Cider vinegar	4 tsp.	20 mL
Water	2 tbsp.	30 mL
Worcestershire sauce	1 tsp.	5 mL
Granulated sugar	¼ cup	60 mL
Ground ginger	¼ tsp.	1 mL
Celery salt	¼ tsp.	1 mL
Cayenne pepper	¼ tsp.	1 mL
Canned pineapple tidbits, with juice	8 oz.	227 mL
Cooking oil	1 tbsp.	15 mL
Pork tenderloin, cut lengthwise and thinly sliced	¾ lb.	340 g
Thinly sliced onion	⅓ cup	75 mL
Grated orange peel	2 tsp.	10 mL

Stir soy sauce into cornstarch in medium bowl. Add next 7 ingredients. Stir. Add pineapple tidbits with juice. Set aside.

Heat wok or frying pan on medium-high. Add cooking oil. Add pork slices. Stir-fry for 2 minutes until no pink remains in pork. Add onion and orange peel. Stir-fry for 1 minute. Stir cornstarch mixture. Stir into pork mixture until boiling and thickened. Serves 4.

1 serving: 232 Calories; 5.7 g Total Fat; 303 mg Sodium; 19 g Protein; 27 g Carbohydrate; 1 g Dietary Fiber

1. Glazed Claret Ham, page 96
2. Fruity Pork And Rice, page 87

Props Courtesy Of: Chintz & Company
The Bay

Pork

Chinese Pork

Excellent served over hot steamed noodles.

Reserved pineapple juice		
Cornstarch	4 tsp.	20 mL
White vinegar	2 tbsp.	30 mL
Brown sugar, packed	2 tbsp.	30 mL
Low-sodium soy sauce	1 tbsp.	15 mL
Salt	½ tsp.	2 mL
Canned pineapple tidbits, drained and juice reserved	8 oz.	227 mL
Cooking oil	1 tbsp.	15 mL
Pork tenderloin, halved lengthwise and thinly sliced	¾ lb.	340 g
Cooking oil	1 tsp.	5 mL
Medium onion, thinly sliced	1	1
Medium green pepper, cut into strips	1	1

Stir reserved pineapple juice into cornstarch in medium bowl. Add vinegar, brown sugar, soy sauce and salt. Stir. Add pineapple tidbits. Set aside.

Heat wok or frying pan on medium-high. Add first amount of cooking oil. Add pork slices. Stir-fry until no pink remains. Transfer to bowl.

Add second amount of cooking oil to hot wok. Add onion and green pepper. Stir-fry until tender-crisp. Add pork. Stir pineapple mixture. Stir into pork mixture until boiling and thickened. Serves 4.

1 serving: 228 Calories; 6.8 g Total Fat; 542 mg Sodium; 19 g Protein; 23 g Carbohydrate; 1 g Dietary Fiber

1. Three Seafood Fry, page 79
2. Dilled Snapper Fry, page 67
3. Shrimp Creole, page 75

Props Courtesy Of: Chintz & Company
Le Gnome

Apricot Pork Stir-Fry

Try this instead of the usual apple and pork.

APRICOT SAUCE

Low-sodium soy sauce	3 tbsp.	50 mL
Cornstarch	1 tbsp.	15 mL
Apricot jam	½ cup	125 mL
Apple cider vinegar	1½ tbsp.	25 mL
Dry mustard	1 tbsp.	15 mL
Granulated sugar	2 tsp.	10 mL
Minced ginger (in bottle)	¼ tsp.	1 mL
Cooking oil	1 tbsp.	15 mL
Pork tenderloin, cut into ⅛ inch (3 mm) thin strips	¾ lb.	340 g
Chopped dried apricots	⅔ cup	150 mL
Hot water	1 cup	250 mL
Cooking oil	1 tsp.	5 mL
Medium red onion, sliced	1	1
Medium green pepper, cut into 1 inch (2.5 cm) squares	1	1
Medium carrot, cut into matchsticks	1	1

Apricot Sauce: Stir soy sauce into cornstarch in small bowl. Add next 5 ingredients. Stir. Set aside.

Heat wok or frying pan on medium-high. Add first amount of cooking oil. Add pork strips. Stir-fry until no pink remains in pork. Transfer to bowl.

Add apricots and hot water to hot wok. Cover. Steam for 10 minutes. Drain. Add apricot to pork in bowl.

Add second amount of cooking oil to hot wok. Add red onion, green pepper and carrot. Stir-fry for 4 to 5 minutes until tender-crisp. Add pork and apricot. Stir cornstarch mixture. Stir into pork mixture until boiling and thickened. Makes 4 cups (1 L). Serves 4.

1 serving: 369 Calories; 7.7 g Total Fat; 528 mg Sodium; 22 g Protein; 56 g Carbohydrate; 4 g Dietary Fiber

Pork

Exotic Pork Meatballs

Serve with cocktail picks and Plum Sauce, page 114.

Large egg	1	1
Low-sodium soy sauce	1 tbsp.	15 mL
Apple (or orange) juice	1 tbsp.	15 mL
Green onions, chopped	2	2
Granulated sugar	1 tsp.	5 mL
Salt	³/₄ tsp.	4 mL
All-purpose flour	2 tbsp.	30 mL
Onion powder	¹/₈ tsp.	0.5 mL
Fine dry bread crumbs	¹/₃ cup	75 mL
Lean ground pork	¹/₂ lb.	225 g
Canned broken shrimp, drained, rinsed and mashed	4 oz.	113 g
Cooking oil	1 tbsp.	15 mL

Beat egg with fork in small bowl. Add next 8 ingredients. Stir.

Add ground pork and shrimp. Mix well. Shape into 1 inch (2.5 cm) balls.

Heat wok or frying pan on medium-high. Add cooking oil. Add meatballs. Stir-fry until browned all over and cooked through. Makes 36.

3 meatballs: 71 Calories; 2.8 g Total Fat; 277 mg Sodium; 7 g Protein; 4 g Carbohydrate; trace Dietary Fiber

---

Paré Pointer

Don't agree to go door–to–door to collect for a new community swimming pool. The last person donated a glass of water.

Stir-Fried Ribs

These ribs are superb! Makes an excellent appetizer dish too.

Pork spareribs, separated and cut into 1 inch (2.5 cm) lengths	2¼ lbs.	1 kg
Water	2 cups	500 mL
Low-sodium soy sauce	¼ cup	60 mL
Salt	¾ tsp.	4 mL
Sherry (or alcohol-free sherry)	2 tbsp.	30 mL
Granulated sugar	1 tsp.	5 mL

Combine spareribs, water, soy sauce and salt in wok. Stir. Bring to a boil. Cover. Simmer for 1½ to 2 hours until tender.

Remove cover. Stir in sherry and sugar. Turn heat to medium-high. Stir-fry for about 10 minutes until liquid is evaporated. Serves 4.

1 serving: 317 Calories; 22.2 g Total Fat; 1249 mg Sodium; 24 g Protein; 3 g Carbohydrate; 0 g Dietary Fiber

Instant Stir-Fry

Combines instant rice with vegetables and bacon.

Bacon slices, diced	8	8
Diced onion	1 cup	250 mL
Frozen peas	2 cups	500 mL
Tomato juice	2 cups	500 mL
Seasoned salt	¼ tsp.	1 mL
Salt	¼ tsp.	1 mL
Pepper	¼ tsp.	1 mL
Instant rice	2 cups	500 mL

Heat wok or frying pan on medium-high. Add bacon and onion. Stir-fry for about 3 minutes until onion is soft.

Add frozen peas. Stir-fry for 2 minutes.

Add remaining 5 ingredients. Stir until boiling. Cover. Remove from heat. Let stand for 5 minutes. Makes 6 cups (1.5 L). Serves 6.

1 serving: 359 Calories; 17.8 g Total Fat; 753 mg Sodium; 9 g Protein; 41 g Carbohydrate; 4 g Dietary Fiber

Pork

Ginger Pork And Peppers

Spicy pork with dark glossy sauce.

Water	3 tbsp.	50 mL
Cornstarch	1 tbsp.	15 mL
Low-sodium soy sauce	3 tbsp.	50 mL
Chicken bouillon powder	1 tsp.	5 mL
Garlic powder	¼ tsp.	1 mL
Cooking oil	1 tbsp.	15 mL
Boneless pork chops, cut into thin slices	¾ lb.	340 g
Finely grated gingerroot	½ tsp.	2 mL
Medium orange pepper, cut into strips	1	1
Canned sliced water chestnuts, drained	8 oz.	227 mL
Cherry tomatoes, halved	8	8

Stir water into cornstarch in small cup. Add soy sauce, bouillon powder and garlic powder. Set aside.

Heat wok or frying pan on medium-high. Add cooking oil. Add pork slices and ginger. Stir-fry until no pink remains in pork. Transfer to bowl.

Add orange pepper to hot wok. Stir-fry for about 2 minutes. Add pork and ginger. Stir cornstarch mixture. Stir into pork mixture until boiling and thickened.

Add water chestnuts and tomato halves. Stir to heat through. Makes 4 cups (1 L). Serves 4.

1 serving: 210 Calories; 8.7 g Total Fat; 692 mg Sodium; 21 g Protein; 12 g Carbohydrate; 1 g Dietary Fiber

Pictured on page 54 and back cover.

Paré Pointer

When asked if he has lived here all his life, he replied, "Not yet."

Glazed Claret Ham

Salty ham, sweet vegetables and claret wine make a delicious combination.

Cooking oil	1 tbsp.	15 mL
Small butternut squash (1¼ lbs., 560 g), cut into matchsticks before peeling	1	1
Fresh pea pods (or 6 oz., 170 g, frozen, partially thawed)	2 cups	500 mL
Canned whole baby corn, drained, cut in half if too long	14 oz.	398 mL
Granulated sugar	6 tbsp.	100 mL
Claret wine (or alcohol-free wine)	½ cup	125 mL
Ham slice, cut into ¼ inch (6 mm) thin strips	¾ lb.	340 g
Water	2 tsp.	10 mL
Cornstarch	2 tsp.	10 mL

Heat wok or frying pan on medium-high. Add cooking oil. Add squash and peas pods. Stir-fry for 6 to 7 minutes. Transfer to bowl.

Add baby corn to bowl.

Add sugar and wine to hot wok. Stir until sugar is dissolved. Boil for 1 minute until foamy and thickened.

Add ham. Stir to coat. Stir in vegetables.

Stir water into cornstarch in small cup. Stir into ham mixture until boiling and thickened. Makes 6 cups (1.5 L). Serves 4.

1 serving: 414 Calories; 13 g Total Fat; 1133 mg Sodium; 21 g Protein; 53 g Carbohydrate; 6 g Dietary Fiber

Pictured on page 89.

Paré Pointer

Man's makeup actually works backwards. When you pat him on the back, his head swells.

Pork

Spicy Ham Stir-Fry

This is nice and crisp. Loaded with vegetables.

Orange marmalade	¼ cup	60 mL
Frozen concentrated orange juice	2 tbsp.	30 mL
Raisins	2 tbsp.	30 mL
Prepared mustard	1½ tsp.	7 mL
Ground cloves	⅛ tsp.	0.5 mL
Ground ginger	⅛ tsp.	0.5 mL
Drops of hot pepper sauce	3	3
Cooking oil	2 tsp.	10 mL
Ham slice (½ inch, 12 mm, thick), cut into ½ inch (12 mm) cubes	¾ lb.	340 g
Cooking oil	2 tsp.	10 mL
Cauliflower florets	2 cups	500 mL
Medium carrot, thinly sliced on diagonal	1	1
Frozen pea pods, partially thawed (or 2 cups, 500 mL, fresh)	6 oz.	170 g

Stir first 7 ingredients in small bowl. Set aside.

Heat wok or frying pan on medium-high. Add first amount of cooking oil. Add ham. Stir-fry until browned. Transfer to bowl.

Add second amount of cooking oil to hot wok. Add cauliflower and carrot. Stir-fry for 3 minutes.

Add pea pods. Stir-fry for 1 minute. Stir marmalade mixture. Add to vegetables. Add ham. Stir to heat through and coat ham. Serves 4.

1 serving: 323 Calories; 14 g Total Fat; 1168 mg Sodium; 18 g Protein; 33 g Carbohydrate; 3 g Dietary Fiber

 tip *If you prefer your vegetables softer than what most stir-fry recipes will produce, there are two methods you can use. Boil or steam the vegetables before adding to the wok. Or stir-fry the vegetables for 2 to 4 minutes then add 3 to 4 tbsp. (50 to 60 mL) water. Cover. Steam for 2 to 3 minutes until softened to your preference.*

Pasta Carbonara

Be different—try making your carbonara in a wok.

Linguine pasta or spaghetti	8 oz.	225 g
Boiling water	3 qts.	3 L
Cooking oil (optional)	1 tbsp.	15 mL
Salt	2 tsp.	10 mL
Large eggs	3	3
Milk	2 tbsp.	30 mL
Grated Romano (or Parmesan) cheese	⅓ cup	75 mL
Bacon slices, diced	12	12
Chopped onion	½ cup	125 mL

Cook pasta in boiling water, cooking oil and salt in large uncovered pot or Dutch oven for 11 to 13 minutes until tender but firm. Drain. Return pasta to pot. Cover to keep warm.

Beat eggs and milk in medium bowl until smooth. Add cheese. Beat well.

Heat wok or frying pan on medium-high. Add bacon and onion. Stir-fry until bacon is cooked and onion is soft. Drain. Add pasta. Stir to heat through. Transfer to large bowl. Add egg mixture, stirring well so eggs will cook in hot pasta. Makes 5 cups (1.25 L). Serves 4.

1 serving: 424 Calories; 16.8 g Total Fat; 479 mg Sodium; 21 g Protein; 45 g Carbohydrate; 2 g Dietary Fiber

Wieners And Beans

A pleasant and interesting variation of kids' favorite.

Cooking oil	2 tsp.	10 mL
Lean ground beef	½ lb.	225 g
Frozen baby carrots, left whole	1 lb.	500 g
Sliced fresh mushrooms	1 cup	250 mL
Wieners, cut into 6 pieces each	1 lb.	454 g
Ketchup	2 tbsp.	30 mL
Canned beans in tomato sauce	2 x 14 oz.	2 x 398 mL

(continued on next page)

Pork

Heat wok or frying pan on medium-high. Add cooking oil. Add ground beef, frozen carrots and mushrooms. Stir-fry for 5 to 6 minutes until carrots are tender-crisp and no pink remains in beef. Drain.

Add wiener pieces. Stir-fry for 2 to 3 minutes to brown slightly.

Add ketchup and beans in sauce. Stir to heat through. Makes 8 cups (2 L). Serves 6.

1 serving: 473 Calories; 27.4 g Total Fat; 1512 mg Sodium; 23 g Protein; 38 g Carbohydrate; 12 g Dietary Fiber

Sausages And Beans

A satisfying dish that is quick and easy to prepare.

Cooking oil	2 tsp.	10 mL
Green pepper slivers	½ cup	125 mL
Red pepper slivers	½ cup	125 mL
Yellow pepper slivers	½ cup	125 mL
Chopped onion	½ cup	125 mL
Small cooking apple, peeled and chopped	1	1
Brown and serve sausages, cut into 3 pieces each	¾ lb.	340 g
Canned beans in tomato sauce	2 x 14 oz.	2 x 398 mL

Heat wok or frying pan on medium-high. Add cooking oil. Add pepper slivers, onion and apple. Stir-fry for about 2 minutes.

Add sausage. Stir-fry for 2 minutes.

Add beans in sauce. Stir to heat through. Makes 6 cups (1.5 L). Serves 4.

1 serving: 611 Calories; 37.7 g Total Fat; 1412 mg Sodium; 21 g Protein; 54 g Carbohydrate; 18 g Dietary Fiber

---

Paré Pointer
If that's a real watch-dog, it should go tick-tick before it goes woof-woof.

Pork And Green Beans

This dish gives a whole new meaning to "Pork And Beans." Colorful and delicious.

White vinegar	¼ cup	60 mL
Cornstarch	2 tbsp.	30 mL
Chicken bouillon powder	1 tsp.	5 mL
Granulated sugar	1 cup	250 mL
Low-sodium soy sauce	1 tbsp.	15 mL
Canned pineapple tidbits, with juice	8 oz.	227 mL
Cooking oil	1 tbsp.	15 mL
Boneless pork loin, cut into thin strips	¾ lb.	340 g
Frozen cut green beans, partially thawed	1 lb.	454 g
Canned whole baby corn, drained	14 oz.	398 mL

Stir vinegar into cornstarch in small bowl. Add bouillon powder, sugar and soy sauce. Stir together well. Stir in pineapple with juice. Set aside.

Heat wok or frying pan on medium-high. Add cooking oil. Add pork strips. Stir-fry until no pink remains in pork. Transfer to bowl.

Add green beans to hot wok. Stir-fry for 5 to 7 minutes until tender-crisp.

Add baby corn. Stir to heat through. Add pork. Stir cornstarch mixture. Stir into pork mixture until boiling and thickened. Serves 4.

1 serving: 506 Calories; 9 g Total Fat; 573 mg Sodium; 23 g Protein; 89 g Carbohydrate; 4 g Dietary Fiber

 Stir-fry is an economical way to serve a lot of people. Plan about 3 oz. (85 g) of raw meat per serving (rather than the suggested 4 oz. (113 g). Supplement with inexpensive vegetables such as carrot and onion. Then add smaller amounts of the more costly or seasonal veggies. Serve with a large bowl of hot rice or pasta and a basket of rolls.

Hot Lettuce Salad

Great on a cold day!

Hard margarine (or butter)	1 tbsp.	15 mL
Chopped onion	½ cup	125 mL
Chopped green, red and yellow peppers	½ cup	125 mL
Medium radishes, slivered	2	2
Medium tomato, seeded and chopped	1	1
Dried sweet basil	½ tsp.	2 mL
Salt	½ tsp.	2 mL
Pepper	⅛ tsp.	0.5 mL
Small head of lettuce, chopped (about 4 cups, 1 L, lightly packed)	1	1

Heat wok or frying pan on medium. Add margarine to melt. Add onion, peppers and radish. Stir-fry on medium-high until tender-crisp.

Add tomato, basil, salt and pepper. Stir to coat.

Add lettuce. Stir-fry until hot but not wilted. Makes 4 cups (1 L).

1 cup (250 mL): 60 Calories; 3.2 g Total Fat; 387 mg Sodium; 2 g Protein; 7 g Carbohydrate; 2 g Dietary Fiber

Pictured on page 54 and back cover.

Stir-Fried Lettuce

Moist and very tasty. Who would have thought to stir-fry lettuce! An excellent side dish.

Cooking oil	1½ tsp.	7 mL
Seasoned salt	½ tsp.	2 mL
Pepper, just a pinch		
Onion powder, just a pinch		
Medium head of iceberg lettuce, torn or cut into large pieces	1	1

Heat wok or frying pan on medium-high. Add cooking oil. Add seasoned salt, pepper and onion powder. Stir quickly.

Add lettuce. Stir-fry for 1 to 2 minutes until lettuce is hot but not wilted. Immediately remove from heat. Serves 4.

1 serving: 33 Calories; 1.9 g Total Fat; 182 mg Sodium; 1 g Protein; 3 g Carbohydrate; 1 g Dietary Fiber

Shrimp Salad

This makes an attractive luncheon salad. Serve with dinner rolls.

Cooking oil	1 tbsp.	15 mL
Medium onion, chopped	1	1
Chopped green pepper	½ cup	125 mL
Chopped celery	1 cup	250 mL
Chopped fresh mushrooms	1 cup	250 mL
Canned medium shrimp, rinsed and drained	2 x 4 oz.	2 x 113 g
Salt, sprinkle		
Pepper, sprinkle		
Light salad dressing (or mayonnaise)	½ cup	125 mL
Worcestershire sauce	1 tsp.	5 mL
Shredded lettuce, lightly packed	4 cups	1 L
Sliced almonds, toasted	½ cup	125 mL

Heat wok or frying pan on medium-high. Add cooking oil. Add onion, green pepper, celery and mushrooms. Stir-fry until celery is tender-crisp.

Add shrimp. Sprinkle with salt and pepper. Add salad dressing and Worcestershire sauce. Stir just until hot.

Spread lettuce on platter or 4 individual plates. Spoon shrimp mixture over lettuce. Sprinkle with almonds. Serves 4.

1 serving: 287 Calories; 18.8 g Total Fat; 366 mg Sodium; 16 g Protein; 11 g Carbohydrate; 4 g Dietary Fiber

Seafood Salad

Pretty colors—shades of greens and pinks. This is ready in 5 minutes!

Cooking oil	1 tbsp.	15 mL
Medium green pepper, chopped	1	1
Chopped onion	½ cup	125 mL
Chopped celery	1 cup	250 mL
Canned crabmeat, drained and cartilage removed	4.2 oz.	120 g
Canned small shrimp, rinsed and drained	4 oz.	113 g

(continued on next page)

Salads

Light salad dressing (or mayonnaise)	¾ cup	175 mL
Worcestershire sauce	1 tsp.	5 mL
Dill weed	½ tsp.	2 mL
Salt	½ tsp.	2 mL
Pepper	½ tsp.	2 mL
Shredded lettuce	4 cups	1 L

Heat wok or frying pan on medium-high. Add cooking oil. Add green pepper, onion and celery. Stir-fry for 1 minute until soft.

Add crabmeat and shrimp. Stir-fry for 1 minute until hot.

Add next 5 ingredients. Stir only to heat through.

Divide lettuce among 4 individual plates. Divide seafood mixture over top. Serves 4.

1 serving: 244 Calories; 15.8 g Total Fat; 964 mg Sodium; 12 g Protein; 7 g Carbohydrate; 2 g Dietary Fiber

Steak Sandwiches

Quick and easy to put together. Sure to please.

Cooking oil	1 tbsp.	15 mL
Sirloin steak, sliced into ⅛ inch (3 mm) thin strips	¾ lb.	340 g
Small red onion, sliced	1	1
Slivered green or red pepper	½ cup	125 mL
Worcestershire sauce	1½ tsp.	7 mL
Salt	½ tsp.	2 mL
Pepper	¼ tsp.	1 mL
Kaiser (or other) buns, split and buttered	6	6
Grated medium Cheddar cheese	½ cup	125 mL

Heat wok or frying pan on medium-high. Add cooking oil. Add beef strips. Stir-fry for 3 minutes. Add red onion and green pepper strips. Stir-fry for 2 minutes.

Sprinkle with Worcestershire sauce, salt and pepper. Stir well.

Spoon beef mixture onto bottom halves of buns. Sprinkle cheese over beef mixture. Cover with top halves of buns. Makes 6.

1 sandwich: 330 Calories; 13.3 g Total Fat; 690 mg Sodium; 20 g Protein; 32 g Carbohydrate; 1 g Dietary Fiber

Sandwiches

Beef Fajitas

Once the chopping is done, the rest is fast and easy. Set everything out so everyone can assemble their own.

Flour tortillas (6 inch, 15 cm, size)	8	8
Sirloin steak, sliced into ⅛ inch (3 mm) thin strips	¾ lb.	340 g
Lemon juice	1 tbsp.	15 mL
Chili powder	½ tsp.	2 mL
Salt	½ tsp.	2 mL
Pepper	¹⁄₁₆ tsp.	0.5 mL
Cooking oil	1 tsp.	5 mL
Medium green pepper, cut into long strips	1	1
Medium red pepper, cut into long strips	1	1
Large onion, cut into long strips	1	1
Cooking oil	1 tbsp.	15 mL
Medium tomatoes, diced	2	2
Grated medium or sharp Cheddar cheese	½ cup	125 mL
Light sour cream	3 tbsp.	50 mL
Salsa	½ cup	125 mL
Shredded lettuce, packed	1 cup	250 mL
Guacamole (optional)	½ cup	125 mL

Sprinkle tortillas with water. Wrap in foil. Place in 275°F (140°C) oven to warm and soften.

Stir steak strips, lemon juice, chili powder, salt and pepper in small bowl. Set aside.

Heat wok or frying pan on medium-high. Add first amount of cooking oil. Add pepper strips and onion. Stir-fry for 4 minutes until soft. Transfer to separate bowl.

Add second amount of cooking oil to hot wok. Add beef strips. Stir-fry for 4 minutes until desired doneness. Add pepper mixture. Stir to heat through.

(continued on next page)

Sandwiches

Place remaining 6 ingredients in separate small bowls. Unwrap tortillas as needed. Lay strips of beef, peppers and onion on each tortilla. Add garnishes from bowls as desired. Roll up bottom end and sides of tortilla around filling. Makes 8.

1 fajita: 237 Calories; 6.4 g Total Fat; 630 mg Sodium; 16 g Protein; 29 g Carbohydrate; 2 g Dietary Fiber

Chicken Fajitas: Substitute ¾ lb. (340 g) chicken strips for the beef.

Pita Fajitas

Cumin, caraway and cilantro bring the flavors of the Middle East and Asia to your table.

Cooking oil	1 tbsp.	15 mL
Sirloin steak, sliced into ⅛ inch (3 mm) thin strips	½ lb.	225 g
Cooking oil	1 tsp.	5 mL
Chopped onion	1 cup	250 mL
Chopped green pepper	½ cup	125 mL
Cumin seed	1 tsp.	5 mL
Caraway seed	½ tsp.	2 mL
Garlic cloves, finely chopped (optional)	2-4	2-4
Canned refried beans	14 oz.	398 mL
Chopped fresh cilantro (or parsley)	2 tbsp.	30 mL
Salt, sprinkle		
Pepper, sprinkle		
Medium tomatoes, diced	2	2
Pita breads (7 inch, 18 cm, size), cut in half crosswise	4	4
Grated medium Cheddar cheese	1 cup	250 mL

Heat wok or frying pan on medium-high. Add first amount of cooking oil. Add beef strips. Stir-fry until desired doneness. Transfer to bowl.

Add second amount of cooking oil to hot wok. Add next 5 ingredients. Stir-fry for 3 minutes.

Add refried beans, cilantro, salt and pepper. Stir until hot.

Add tomato. Add beef. Stir. Divide among 8 pita halves. Sprinkle about 2 tbsp. (30 mL) cheese over each. Makes 8.

1 pita half: 273 Calories; 9.5 g Total Fat; 442 mg Sodium; 17 g Protein; 30 g Carbohydrate; 4 g Dietary Fiber

Sandwiches

Burrito Snacks

Adjust quantity of salsa and cheese to your liking.

Flour tortillas (10 inch, 25 cm, size), sprinkled with water and stacked and wrapped in foil	8	8
Cooking oil	1 tsp.	5 mL
Lean ground beef	¾ lb.	340 g
Chopped onion	1 cup	250 mL
Canned refried beans	14 oz.	398 mL
Canned diced green chilies, with liquid	4 oz.	114 mL
Grated Monterey Jack cheese	1 cup	250 mL
Salsa	½-1 cup	125-250 mL

Sprinkle tortillas with water. Wrap in foil. Place in 275°F (140°C) oven to warm and soften.

Heat wok or frying pan on medium-high. Add cooking oil. Add ground beef and onion. Stir-fry until beef is no longer pink. Drain.

Add refried beans and green chilies with liquid to hot wok. Stir-fry until hot. Place ½ cup (125 mL) beef mixture on each tortilla. Spread bean mixture to within 1 inch (2.5 cm) of edges.

Add cheese and salsa. Roll up, tucking in ends. Makes 8.

1 burrito: 366 Calories; 10 g Total Fat; 936 mg Sodium; 21 g Protein; 47 g Carbohydrate; 4 g Dietary Fiber

1. Bean Sprouts And Peppers, page 120
2. Mandarin Beef, page 39

Props Courtesy Of: Le Gnome

Sandwiches

Beef Pitas

Once you've assembled the basic pita, you can add to or change the
flavor as you like with toppings such as salsa, sour cream,
grated Cheddar cheese and jalapeño peppers.

Cooking oil	1 tbsp.	15 mL
Lean ground beef	¾ lb.	340 g
Medium red onion, sliced	1	1
Chopped fresh mushrooms	1 cup	250 mL
Tomato slices	16	16
Shredded lettuce	2 cups	500 mL
Pita breads (7 inch, 18 cm, size), cut in half crosswise	4	4

Heat wok or frying pan on medium-high. Add cooking oil. Add ground beef, red onion and mushrooms. Stir-fry until browned. Drain.

Place 2 tomato slices and ¼ cup (60 mL) lettuce in each pita pocket. Spoon in ¼ cup (60 mL) beef mixture. Makes 8.

1 pita: 176 Calories; 5.8 g Total Fat; 123 mg Sodium; 11 g Protein; 19 g Carbohydrate; 1 g Dietary Fiber

1. Pasta Primavera, page 116

Props Courtesy Of: Chintz & Company

Chicken Pitas

Contains rice and eggs—similar to fried rice.

Cooking oil	1 tbsp.	15 mL
Boneless, skinless chicken breast halves (about 2), chopped	½ lb.	225 g
Small onion, thinly sliced	1	1
Sliced fresh mushrooms	½ cup	125 mL
Instant rice	½ cup	125 mL
Water	½ cup	125 mL
Salt	¼ tsp.	1 mL
Large eggs, fork-beaten	2	2
Low-sodium soy sauce	1 tsp.	5 mL
Cranberry sauce	¼ cup	60 mL
Pita breads (7 inch, 18 cm, size), cut in half crosswise	4	4
Fresh bean sprouts	1 cup	250 mL

Heat wok or frying pan on medium-high. Add cooking oil. Add chicken and onion. Stir-fry for 4 minutes.

Add mushrooms. Stir-fry for 1 minute.

Add rice, water and salt. Bring to a boil. Cover. Remove from heat for 5 minutes. Return to heat.

Stir in eggs and soy sauce until eggs are cooked.

Spread cranberry sauce on inside of each pita. Spoon chicken mixture into each pita half. Top with bean sprouts. Makes 8.

1 pita: 193 Calories; 3.8 g Total Fat; 252 mg Sodium; 12 g Protein; 27 g Carbohydrate; 1 g Dietary Fiber

 Many stir-fry recipes call for fresh vegetables, but canned foods may be substituted. A good example is using canned mushrooms in place of fresh ones.

Orange Sauce

Try this with a pork or chicken stir-fry.

Prepared orange juice	½ cup	125 mL
Grated orange peel (not zest)	1 tsp.	5 mL
Low-sodium soy sauce	1 tsp.	5 mL
Lemon juice	1 tsp.	5 mL
Granulated sugar	3 tbsp.	50 mL
Water	2 tbsp.	30 mL
Cornstarch	1 tbsp.	15 mL

Heat first 5 ingredients in small saucepan until boiling.

Stir water into cornstarch in cup. Stir into orange juice mixture until boiling and thickened. Makes ⅔ cup (150 mL).

2 tbsp. (30 mL): 43 Calories; trace Total Fat; 38 mg Sodium; trace Protein; 11 g Carbohydrate; trace Dietary Fiber

Pineapple Sauce

This sweet and sour sauce is good with pork or beef.

White vinegar	2 tbsp.	30 mL
Cornstarch	1 tsp.	5 mL
Low-sodium soy sauce	1 tbsp.	15 mL
Brown sugar, packed	2 tbsp.	30 mL
Onion powder	¼ tsp.	1 mL
Chicken bouillon powder	1 tsp.	5 mL
Canned crushed pineapple, with juice	8 oz.	227 mL

Stir vinegar into cornstarch in small bowl.

Add remaining 5 ingredients. Stir just before adding to hot stir-fry mixture. Makes 1⅓ cups (325 mL).

2 tbsp. (30 mL): 26 Calories; trace Total Fat; 119 mg Sodium; trace Protein; 7 g Carbohydrate; trace Dietary Fiber

Mustard Sauce

If you are stir-frying ham or wieners, you will want to try this sauce.

Granulated sugar	¼ cup	60 mL
Brown sugar, packed	¼ cup	60 mL
Prepared mustard	2 tsp.	10 mL
White vinegar	3 tbsp.	50 mL
Water	⅓ cup	75 mL
Cornstarch	1½ tbsp.	25 mL

Combine first 4 ingredients in small saucepan.

Stir water into cornstarch in cup. Add to saucepan. Heat and stir until boiling and thickened. Makes ½ cup (125 mL).

2 tbsp. (30 mL): 117 Calories; 0.1 g Total Fat; 41 mg Sodium; trace Protein; 30 g Carbohydrate; trace Dietary Fiber

Stir-Fry Sauce

Dark and glossy. Great with any stir-fry combination.

Cornstarch	1 tbsp.	15 mL
Brown sugar, packed	1 tbsp.	15 mL
Ground ginger	¼ tsp.	1 mL
Garlic powder	¼ tsp.	1 mL
Beef bouillon powder	1 tsp.	5 mL
Low-sodium soy sauce	3 tbsp.	50 mL
Apple cider vinegar	1 tbsp.	15 mL
Sherry (or alcohol-free sherry)	1½ tbsp.	25 mL
Water	3 tbsp.	50 mL
Drops of hot pepper sauce	3	3

Measure first 5 ingredients into small bowl. Stir well.

Stir in soy sauce, vinegar, sherry, water and hot pepper sauce until smooth. Stir just before adding to hot stir-fry mixture. Makes ½ cup (125 mL).

2 tbsp. (30 mL): 36 Calories; 0.1 g Total Fat; 595 mg Sodium; 1 g Protein; 7 g Carbohydrate; trace Dietary Fiber

Sauces

Black Currant Sauce

Especially good with chicken and pork.

Cooking oil	1 tbsp.	15 mL
Finely chopped onion	2 tbsp.	30 mL
Garlic clove, finely chopped (or ¼ tsp., 1 mL, powder)	1	1
Prepared mustard	1 tsp.	5 mL
Black currant jelly	⅓ cup	75 mL
Apple cider vinegar	1 tbsp.	15 mL
Salt	⅛ tsp.	0.5 mL
Pepper	⅛ tsp.	0.5 mL
Granulated sugar (optional)	1-2 tsp.	5-10 mL
Water	3 tbsp.	50 mL
Cornstarch	2 tsp.	10 mL

Heat cooking oil in small saucepan. Add onion and garlic. Sauté until browned.

Add next 6 ingredients. Stir. Bring to a boil.

Stir water into cornstarch in cup. Stir into jelly mixture until boiling and thickened. Makes ⅔ cup (150 mL).

2 tbsp. (30 mL): 81 Calories; 2.6 g Total Fat; 81 mg Sodium; trace Protein; 15 g Carbohydrate; trace Dietary Fiber

Variation: Substitute grape jelly for black currant jelly.

Black Bean Sauce

Goes well with a beef and onion stir-fry.

Canned black beans, rinsed and drained	½ cup	125 mL
Water	½ cup	125 mL
Low-sodium soy sauce	½ cup	125 mL
Salt (optional)	½ tsp.	2 mL
Brown sugar, packed	4 tsp.	20 mL
Cornstarch	4 tsp.	20 mL

Measure all 6 ingredients into blender. Process until smooth. Strain into small saucepan to remove bits of skin from black beans. Heat and stir until boiling and thickened. Makes ⅔ cup (150 mL).

2 tbsp. (30 mL): 60 Calories; trace Total Fat; 981 mg Sodium; 4 g Protein; 11 g Carbohydrate; 1 g Dietary Fiber

Smoky Sauce

Especially tasty on lima beans, kidney beans and fish. Experiment with the quantity of liquid smoke.

Sherry (or alcohol-free sherry)	2 tbsp.	30 mL
Cornstarch	1 tbsp.	15 mL
Chicken bouillon powder	1 tsp.	5 mL
Water	½ cup	125 mL
Liquid smoke (start with less)	1 tsp.	5 mL

Stir sherry into cornstarch in small bowl. Add remaining 3 ingredients. Stir just before adding to hot stir-fry mixture. Makes ½ cup (125 mL).

2 tbsp. (30 mL): 15 Calories; 0.1 g Total Fat; 157 mg Sodium; trace Protein; 2 g Carbohydrate; trace Dietary Fiber

Plum Sauce

Good on any meat stir-fry. Also can be used as a dip for appetizers. Excellent with Exotic Pork Meatballs, page 93, or Spring Rolls, page 141.

Jar strained plums (baby food)	4½ oz.	128 mL
Brown sugar, packed	2 tsp.	10 mL
White vinegar	1 tbsp.	15 mL
Ground ginger	⅛ tsp.	0.5 mL
Chili powder	⅛ tsp.	0.5 mL
Salt	⅛ tsp.	0.5 mL

Stir all 6 ingredients together in small bowl. Makes ½ cup (125 mL).

2 tbsp. (30 mL): 33 Calories; 0.1 g Total Fat; 88 mg Sodium; trace Protein; 9 g Carbohydrate; trace Dietary Fiber

 When stir-frying, vegetables are usually added in order of their cooking times. Harder vegetables such as carrots will take longer to cook than mushrooms, for instance. A helpful guide, which will give you an idea of cooking times for most vegetables, is featured on page 8.

Raisin Sauce

A perfect sauce for stir-fried ham.

Raisins	¼ cup	60 mL
Water	½ cup	125 mL
Brown sugar, packed	1 tbsp.	15 mL
Lemon juice (or more to taste)	1 tsp.	5 mL
Water	2 tbsp.	30 mL
Cornstarch	2 tsp.	10 mL

Combine raisins, first amount of water, brown sugar and lemon juice in small saucepan. Heat and stir until simmering. Simmer, stirring often, for 3 minutes.

Stir second amount of water into cornstarch in cup. Stir into raisin mixture until boiling and thickened. Makes ½ cup (125 mL).

2 tbsp. (30 mL): 43 Calories; trace Total Fat; 2 mg Sodium; trace Protein; 11 g Carbohydrate; trace Dietary Fiber

Barbecue Sauce

Add this sauce to stir-fried beef, pork or chicken. Rich looking.

Brown sugar, packed	3 tbsp.	50 mL
Ketchup	1½ tbsp.	25 mL
Fancy molasses	2 tsp.	10 mL
Worcestershire sauce	½ tsp.	2 mL
Low-sodium soy sauce	1 tsp.	5 mL
Prepared mustard	½ tsp.	2 mL
Liquid smoke	⅛ tsp.	0.5 mL
White vinegar	3 tbsp.	50 mL
Salt	⅛ tsp.	0.5 mL
Water	¼ cup	60 mL
Cornstarch	2 tsp.	10 mL

Combine first 9 ingredients in small saucepan. Heat, stirring often, until hot.

Stir water into cornstarch in small bowl. Stir into sauce until boiling and thickened. Makes ½ cup (125 mL).

2 tbsp. (30 mL): 61 Calories; 0.1 g Total Fat; 235 mg Sodium; trace Protein; 16 g Carbohydrate; trace Dietary Fiber

Pasta Primavera

A favorite—made quick and easy! Excellent choice.

Spaghetti, broken into thirds	8 oz.	225 g
Boiling water	2½ qts.	2.5 L
Cooking oil (optional)	1 tbsp.	15 mL
Salt	2 tsp.	10 mL
Skim evaporated milk	1⅓ cups	325 mL
Grated Parmesan cheese	⅔ cup	150 mL
Chopped fresh parsley (or 1 tbsp., 15 mL, dried)	¼ cup	60 mL
Chopped fresh basil (or 1 tbsp., 15 mL, dried)	¼ cup	60 mL
Salt	1 tsp.	5 mL
Pepper	¼ tsp.	1 mL
Cooking oil	1 tbsp.	15 mL
Medium carrots, cut into matchsticks	2	2
Medium onion, thinly sliced	1	1
Thinly sliced celery	½ cup	125 mL
Garlic clove, minced (or ¼ tsp., 1 mL, powder)	1	1
Cooking oil	1 tbsp.	15 mL
Cauliflower florets	1 cup	250 mL
Broccoli florets	1 cup	250 mL
Frozen pea pods, partially thawed (or 2 cups, 500 mL, fresh)	6 oz.	170 g
Zucchini slivers, with peel	1 cup	250 mL
Cherry tomatoes, halved	8	8

Grated Parmesan cheese, sprinkle

Cook spaghetti in boiling water and first amounts of cooking oil and salt in large uncovered pot or Dutch oven for 11 to 13 minutes until tender but firm. Drain. Return spaghetti to pot. Cover to keep hot.

Combine next 6 ingredients in small bowl. Set aside.

Heat wok or frying pan on medium-high. Add second amount of cooking oil. Add carrot, onion, celery and garlic. Stir-fry until soft. Transfer to bowl.

(continued on next page)

Vegetables

Add third amount of cooking oil to hot wok. Add cauliflower and broccoli. Stir-fry for 4 minutes until almost cooked.

Add pea pods and zucchini. Stir-fry for 2 to 3 minutes until tender-crisp. Add carrot mixture.

Add tomato halves and evaporated milk mixture. Stir until heated through. Add spaghetti. Stir.

Sprinkle with Parmesan cheese. Makes 10 cups (2.5 L). Serves 4.

1 serving: 497 Calories; 13.8 g Total Fat; 1158 mg Sodium; 25 g Protein; 69 g Carbohydrate; 7 g Dietary Fiber

Pictured on page 108.

Red Cabbage Fry

Very colorful! Nice and sweet. Stays crunchy.

Apple cider vinegar	3 tbsp.	50 mL
Medium cooking apples (such as McIntosh), peeled and coarsely grated	2	2
Brown sugar, packed	3 tbsp.	50 mL
Ground cloves	1/4 tsp.	1 mL
Dry mustard	1/4 tsp.	1 mL
Red (or alcohol-free red) wine	1/3 cup	75 mL
Cooking oil	1 tbsp.	15 mL
Large head of red cabbage, shredded (about 4 lbs., 1.8 kg)	1	1
Water	3 tbsp.	50 mL
Cornstarch	2 tbsp.	30 mL

Combine first 6 ingredients in small bowl. Set aside.

Heat wok or frying pan on medium-high. Add cooking oil. Add cabbage. Stir-fry until tender-crisp. Reduce heat to medium. Add apple mixture. Stir-fry for 1 minute.

Stir water into cornstarch in cup. Stir into cabbage mixture until boiling and thickened. Makes 6 cups (1.5 L).

1/2 cup (125 mL): 87 Calories; 1.6 g Total Fat; 18 mg Sodium; 2 g Protein; 17 g Carbohydrate; 3 g Dietary Fiber

Cheesy Brussels Sprouts

A tempting way to serve brussels sprouts. Double recipe to serve 4.

Milk	½ cup	125 mL
Cornstarch	1 tbsp.	15 mL
Chicken bouillon powder	1 tsp.	5 mL
Garlic powder	¼ tsp.	1 mL
Ground thyme	⅛ tsp.	0.5 mL
Seasoned salt	½ tsp.	2 mL
Pepper	¼ tsp.	1 mL
White wine (or apple juice)	2 tbsp.	30 mL
Cooking oil	1 tbsp.	15 mL
Chopped fresh mushrooms	1 cup	250 mL
Finely chopped onion	½ cup	125 mL
Frozen brussels sprouts, thawed, halved if large	10 oz.	284 g
Grated Havarti (or mild Cheddar) cheese	1 tbsp.	15 mL

Stir milk into cornstarch in small bowl. Add next 6 ingredients. Stir. Set aside.

Heat wok or frying pan on medium-high. Add cooking oil. Add mushrooms, onion and brussels sprouts. Stir-fry until sprouts are tender-crisp. Stir cornstarch mixture. Stir into vegetable mixture until boiling and thickened.

Sprinkle with cheese. Makes 2 cups (500 mL). Serves 2 generously.

1 serving: 189 Calories; 9.4 g Total Fat; 736 mg Sodium; 8 g Protein; 19 g Carbohydrate; 4 g Dietary Fiber

Pictured on page 126.

Suey Choy Fry

A good method for cooking this cabbage.

Bacon slices, chopped	6	6
Head of suey (or bok) choy, coarsely chopped	1	1
Low-sodium soy sauce	2 tbsp.	30 mL
Water	1 tbsp.	15 mL
Cornstarch	1 tbsp.	15 mL

(continued on next page)

Heat wok or frying pan on medium-high. Add bacon. Stir-fry until almost cooked. Drain off fat, except for about 1 tbsp. (15 mL).

Add suey choy and soy sauce. Stir-fry until wilted and hot. There will be a lot of liquid.

Stir water into cornstarch in cup. Stir into suey choy mixture until boiling and thickened. Serves 4.

1 serving: 86 Calories; 4.9 g Total Fat; 475 mg Sodium; 5 g Protein; 6 g Carbohydrate; 1 g Dietary Fiber

---

Fancy Carrots

Very good. A creamy sauce, just perfect for rice.

All-purpose flour	1 tbsp.	15 mL
Dry mustard	1/8 tsp.	0.5 mL
Salt	1/4 tsp.	1 mL
Celery salt	1/16 tsp.	0.5 mL
Pepper, sprinkle		
Milk	1/2 cup	125 mL
Hard margarine (or butter)	1 tbsp.	15 mL
Dry bread crumbs	1/4 cup	60 mL
Cooking oil	1 tbsp.	15 mL
Thinly sliced carrot coins or slivers	3 cups	750 mL
Sliced onion	2 tbsp.	30 mL
Grated medium or sharp Cheddar cheese	1/2 cup	125 mL

Measure flour, mustard, salt, celery salt and pepper into small bowl. Gradually stir in milk until smooth. Set aside.

Heat margarine and bread crumbs in cup in microwave until margarine is melted. Stir. Set aside.

Heat wok or frying pan on medium-high. Add cooking oil. Add carrot. Stir-fry for 6 to 8 minutes. Add onion. Stir-fry for about 1 minute until tender-crisp. Stir flour mixture. Stir into carrot mixture until boiling and thickened.

Sprinkle with bread crumb mixture and cheese. Serves 4.

1 serving: 206 Calories; 12.2 g Total Fat; 417 mg Sodium; 7 g Protein; 18 g Carbohydrate; 2 g Dietary Fiber

Bean Sprouts And Peppers

Nice ginger taste with a good color mix of red and green.

Cooking oil	2 tsp.	10 mL
Finely grated gingerroot	1 tsp.	5 mL
Medium green pepper, cut into strips	1	1
Medium red pepper, cut into strips	1	1
Salt	½ tsp.	2 mL
Fresh bean sprouts	1½ cups	375 mL
Chicken bouillon powder	1 tsp.	5 mL
Hot water	¼ cup	60 mL

Heat wok or frying pan on medium-high. Add cooking oil. Add ginger, pepper strips and salt. Stir-fry for 2 minutes.

Add bean sprouts. Stir-fry for 1 minute.

Stir bouillon powder into hot water in cup. Add to hot wok. Cover. Cook for 2 to 3 minutes. Makes 2 cups (500 mL). Serves 4.

1 serving: 64 Calories; 3.2 g Total Fat; 508 mg Sodium; 3 g Protein; 8 g Carbohydrate; 2 g Dietary Fiber

Pictured on page 107.

Bean Sprouts Solo: Stir-fry bean sprouts in hot cooking oil for 4 to 5 minutes. Sprinkle with salt and pepper.

Chinese Pea Pods

Soy sauce and sherry make a tasty sauce for this popular stir-fry vegetable.

Low-sodium soy sauce	1 tbsp.	15 mL
Cornstarch	2 tsp.	10 mL
Water	½ cup	125 mL
Sherry (or alcohol-free sherry)	2 tbsp.	30 mL
Chicken bouillon powder	1½ tsp.	7 mL
Granulated sugar	1 tsp.	5 mL
Salt	½ tsp.	2 mL
Cooking oil	1 tbsp.	15 mL
Diced onion	1 cup	250 mL
Fresh pea pods (or 2 x 6 oz., 2 x 170 g, frozen, partially thawed)	4 cups	1 L

(continued on next page)

Stir soy sauce into cornstarch in small bowl. Add next 5 ingredients. Stir. Set aside.

Heat wok or frying pan on medium-high. Add cooking oil. Add onion. Stir-fry until soft.

Add pea pods. Stir-fry for 3 to 5 minutes. Stir cornstarch mixture. Stir into pea pod mixture until boiling and thickened. Serves 4.

1 serving: 101 Calories; 3.9 g Total Fat; 745 mg Sodium; 4 g Protein; 12 g Carbohydrate; 3 g Dietary Fiber

Stuffed Potatoes

Serve these appealing looking potatoes with sour cream.

Small-medium potatoes	4	4
Low-sodium soy sauce	2 tsp.	10 mL
Golden corn syrup	1 tsp.	5 mL
Cooking oil	1 tbsp.	15 mL
Chopped onion	½ cup	125 mL
Grated carrot	⅓ cup	75 mL
Sliced fresh mushrooms	1 cup	250 mL
Green onions, sliced	2	2
Medium tomato, diced	1	1
Grated medium Cheddar cheese	¼ cup	60 mL

Bake potatoes in microwave or regular oven. Keep hot.

Mix soy sauce and corn syrup in cup. Set aside.

Heat wok or frying pan on medium-high. Add cooking oil. Add onion and carrot. Stir-fry until soft.

Add mushrooms. Stir-fry until golden.

Add green onion and tomato. Add soy sauce mixture. Stir. Cut potatoes in half lengthwise. Remove most of pulp. Mash pulp. Put back into potato. Spoon about 2 tbsp. (30 mL) mushroom mixture over each half.

Sprinkle each with about 1½ tsp. (7 mL) cheese. Makes 8.

1 stuffed potato half: 156 Calories; 3.2 g Total Fat; 88 mg Sodium; 4 g Protein; 29 g Carbohydrate; 3 g Dietary Fiber

Glazed Carrots

Orange juice adds a bit of zest. Carrots are shiny with glaze.

Prepared orange juice	1/3 cup	75 mL
Cornstarch	1½ tsp.	7 mL
Granulated sugar	1 tbsp.	15 mL
Ground ginger	¼ tsp.	1 mL
Salt	¼ tsp.	1 mL
Cooking oil	1 tbsp.	15 mL
Thin carrot coins or slivers	3 cups	750 mL
Hard margarine (or butter), optional	1 tbsp.	15 mL
Toasted sesame seeds, for garnish	1 tbsp.	15 mL

Stir orange juice into cornstarch in small bowl. Add sugar, ginger and salt. Stir. Set aside.

Heat wok or frying pan on medium-high. Add cooking oil. Add carrot. Stir-fry for about 7 minutes until tender-crisp. Stir cornstarch mixture. Stir into carrot mixture until boiling and thickened.

Add margarine. Stir to melt. Sprinkle with sesame seeds. Makes 2½ cups (625 mL). Serves 4.

1 serving: 94 Calories; 3.6 g Total Fat; 200 mg Sodium; 1 g Protein; 15 g Carbohydrate; 2 g Dietary Fiber

Pictured on page 126.

Supreme Broccoli

Bright green and glossy. Broccoli at its best.

Water	6 tbsp.	100 mL
Cornstarch	1 tsp.	5 mL
Chicken bouillon powder	1 tsp.	5 mL
Granulated sugar	½ tsp.	2 mL
Salt	½ tsp.	2 mL
Pepper, sprinkle		
Cooking oil	1 tbsp.	15 mL
Sliced broccoli (florets and peeled stems, about 7 cups, 1.75 L)	1¼ lbs.	560 g
Garlic clove, minced (or ¼ tsp., 1 mL, powder)	1	1

(continued on next page)

Vegetables

Stir water into cornstarch in small bowl. Add next 4 ingredients. Stir. Set aside.

Heat wok or frying pan on medium-high. Add cooking oil. Add broccoli and garlic. Stir-fry for 3 to 4 minutes. Stir cornstarch mixture. Stir into broccoli mixture until boiling and thickened. Makes 5 cups (1.25 L). Serves 4.

1 serving: 78 Calories; 4.1 g Total Fat; 540 mg Sodium; 4 g Protein; 9 g Carbohydrate; 3 g Dietary Fiber

Beets And Onions

A natural go-together.

Lemon juice	1 tbsp.	15 mL
Parsley flakes	1 tsp.	5 mL
Salt	¼ tsp.	1 mL
Cooking oil	1 tbsp.	15 mL
Peeled and diced fresh beets	2 cups	500 mL
Small red onion, sliced	1	1
Hard margarine (or butter)	1 tbsp.	15 mL

Stir lemon juice, parsley and salt in small bowl. Set aside.

Heat wok or frying pan on medium-high. Add cooking oil. Add beets. Stir-fry for 4 to 5 minutes.

Add red onion. Stir-fry for about 1 minute.

Stir in lemon juice mixture. Add margarine. Stir to melt. Serves 4.

1 serving: 92 Calories; 6.5 g Total Fat; 249 mg Sodium; 1 g Protein; 8 g Carbohydrate; 2 g Dietary Fiber

Pictured on page 125.

Paré Pointer
The easiest way to make a bandstand is simply to take away their chairs.

Stir-Fried Peas

Fast and fancy.

Water	½ cup	125 mL
Cornstarch	2 tsp.	10 mL
Chicken bouillon powder	1 tsp.	5 mL
Salt	⅛ tsp.	0.5 mL
Pepper	1/16 tsp.	0.5 mL
Bacon slices, cut into ½ inch (12 mm) pieces	2	2
Thinly shredded lettuce	1½ cups	375 mL
Frozen peas	2 cups	500 mL
Green onions, sliced	2	2
Canned sliced water chestnuts, drained	8 oz.	227 mL

Stir water into cornstarch in small bowl. Add bouillon powder, salt and pepper. Mix. Set aside.

Stir-fry bacon in hot wok or frying pan for about 2 minutes until almost cooked.

Add lettuce, frozen peas, green onion and water chestnuts. Stir-fry for 1 to 2 minutes. Stir cornstarch mixture. Stir into pea mixture until boiling and thickened. Serves 4.

1 serving: 158 Calories; 7 g Total Fat; 425 mg Sodium; 6 g Protein; 18 g Carbohydrate; 4 g Dietary Fiber

1. Chicken 'N' Stuffing, page 50
2. Beets And Onions, page 123

Props Courtesy Of: Chintz & Company
The Bay

Green Bean Stir-Fry

Tender-crisp veggies with crunchy almonds.

Low-sodium soy sauce	1 tbsp.	15 mL
Salt	¼ tsp.	1 mL
Garlic powder	¼ tsp.	1 mL
Ground ginger	⅛ tsp.	0.5 mL
Slivered almonds	¼ cup	60 mL
Cooking oil	1 tbsp.	15 mL
Frozen cut green beans, partially thawed	2 cups	500 mL
Sliced fresh mushrooms	1 cup	250 mL
Frozen kernel corn	1 cup	250 mL
Green onions, sliced	4	4

Stir first 5 ingredients together in small bowl. Set aside.

Heat wok or frying pan on medium-high. Add cooking oil. Add green beans. Stir-fry for about 4 minutes.

Add mushrooms, frozen corn and green onion. Stir-fry for 2 minutes. Add soy sauce mixture. Stir until hot. Serves 4.

1 serving: 150 Calories; 8.6 g Total Fat; 334 mg Sodium; 5 g Protein; 17 g Carbohydrate; 4 g Dietary Fiber

1. Cheesy Brussels Sprouts, page 118
2. Glazed Carrots, page 122

Props Courtesy Of: Eaton's
X/S Wares

Mushroom Mixture

This satisfies the desire for a mushroom feast.

Water	1 tbsp.	15 mL
Cornstarch	1 tsp.	5 mL
Low-sodium soy sauce	2 tbsp.	30 mL
Granulated sugar	1 tsp.	5 mL
White vinegar	1 tsp.	5 mL
Ground ginger (or ⅛ tsp., 0.5 mL, minced)	¹⁄₁₆ tsp.	0.5 mL
Garlic powder	¹⁄₁₆ tsp.	0.5 mL
Cooking oil	1 tbsp.	15 mL
Small whole fresh mushrooms, halved or quartered if larger	4 cups	1 L
Very thinly sliced onion	½ cup	125 mL
Thinly sliced celery	½ cup	125 mL
Sesame seeds, toasted	1 tbsp.	15 mL

Stir water into cornstarch in cup. Add next 5 ingredients. Stir. Set aside.

Heat wok or frying pan on medium-high. Add cooking oil. Add mushrooms, onion and celery. Stir-fry for 4 to 5 minutes until soft and golden. Stir cornstarch mixture. Stir into mushroom mixture until boiling and slightly thickened.

Sprinkle with sesame seeds. Makes 2½ cups (625 mL). Serves 4.

1 serving: 84 Calories; 5 g Total Fat; 331 mg Sodium; 3 g Protein; 8 g Carbohydrate; 2 g Dietary Fiber

 tip   *Take the opportunity to chop extra onions, green peppers and carrots when you have the time. Then store the chopped vegetables in separate containers in the refrigerator to have on hand for your next stir-fry!*

Vegetables

Mixed Vegetables

Cauliflower, carrots and baby corn make a most colorful array in a bowl.

Water	½ cup	125 mL
Cornstarch	1 tbsp.	15 mL
Oyster sauce	2 tbsp.	30 mL
Chicken bouillon powder	1 tsp.	5 mL
Low-sodium soy sauce	1 tsp.	5 mL
Granulated sugar	1 tsp.	5 mL
Salt	½ tsp.	2 mL
Ground ginger, scant	¼ tsp.	1 mL
Cooking oil	1 tbsp.	15 mL
Baby carrots, thinly sliced	1 lb.	454 g
Small head of cauliflower, cut up into small pieces	1	1
Canned whole baby corn, drained	14 oz.	398 mL

Stir water into cornstarch in small bowl. Add next 6 ingredients. Stir. Set aside.

Heat wok or frying pan on medium-high. Add cooking oil. Add carrot. Stir-fry for 3 to 4 minutes.

Add cauliflower. Stir-fry for 4 to 5 minutes.

Add baby corn. Stir cornstarch mixture. Stir into vegetable mixture until boiling and thickened. Serves 8.

1 serving: 101 Calories; 2.3 g Total Fat; 766 mg Sodium; 3 g Protein; 20 g Carbohydrate; 4 g Dietary Fiber

Paré Pointer
Little Joey didn't know how old his Grandpa was. He just knew they'd had him for a long time.

Carrots And Cabbage

Delicious. Sweet ginger sauce complements this dish.

Water	⅓ cup	75 mL
Cornstarch	1 tbsp.	15 mL
White vinegar	3 tbsp.	50 mL
Brown sugar, packed	¼ cup	60 mL
Low-sodium soy sauce	1 tsp.	5 mL
Ground ginger	½ tsp.	2 mL
Salt	½ tsp.	2 mL
Cooking oil	2 tsp.	10 mL
Medium carrots, cut into thin coins or on diagonal into thin slices	3	3
Chopped red cabbage	1½ cups	375 mL
Green onions, cut into 1 inch (2.5 cm) pieces	3	3

Stir water into cornstarch in small bowl. Add next 5 ingredients. Stir. Set aside.

Heat wok or frying pan on medium-high. Add cooking oil. Add carrot. Stir-fry for 3 to 4 minutes.

Add cabbage. Stir-fry for 1 minute.

Add green onion. Stir-fry for 1 minute. Stir cornstarch mixture. Stir into carrot mixture until boiling and thickened. Makes 3 cups (750 mL). Serves 4.

1 serving: 121 Calories; 2.5 g Total Fat; 421 mg Sodium; 1 g Protein; 25 g Carbohydrate; 2 g Dietary Fiber

Pictured on page 143.

Harvard Beets

A colorful side dish.

Water	¼ cup	60 mL
Cornstarch	1 tbsp.	15 mL
White vinegar	¼ cup	60 mL
Granulated sugar	⅓ cup	75 mL
Salt	½ tsp.	2 mL
Cooking oil	1 tbsp.	15 mL
Peeled and slivered beets	4 cups	1 L

(continued on next page)

Vegetables

Stir water into cornstarch in small bowl. Add vinegar, sugar and salt. Stir. Set aside.

Heat wok or frying pan on medium-high. Add cooking oil. Add beets. Stir-fry for 9 to 10 minutes until tender-crisp. Stir cornstarch mixture. Stir into beet mixture until boiling and thickened. Makes 2 cups (500 mL). Serves 4.

1 serving: 163 Calories; 3.6 g Total Fat; 428 mg Sodium; 2 g Protein; 32 g Carbohydrate; 4 g Dietary Fiber

Lima Beans And Mushrooms

A good way to serve lima beans.

Water	¼ cup	60 mL
Cornstarch	1 tbsp.	15 mL
Milk	¼ cup	60 mL
Sherry (or alcohol-free sherry)	2 tsp.	10 mL
Chicken bouillon powder	½ tsp.	2 mL
Salt	⅛ tsp.	0.5 mL
Pepper	⅛ tsp.	0.5 mL
Hard margarine (or butter)	2 tsp.	10 mL
Dry bread crumbs	2 tbsp.	30 mL
Cooking oil	1 tbsp.	15 mL
Frozen lima beans	2 cups	500 mL
Small whole fresh mushrooms, halved or quartered if larger	2 cups	500 mL

Stir water into cornstarch in small bowl. Add next 5 ingredients. Stir. Set aside.

Melt margarine with bread crumbs in wok or frying pan. Stir-fry to brown. Transfer to saucer.

Heat wok or frying pan on medium-high. Add cooking oil. Add frozen lima beans. Stir-fry for about 3 minutes until showing signs of browning. Transfer to bowl.

Add mushrooms to hot wok. Stir-fry for about 2 minutes until golden. Add lima beans. Stir cornstarch mixture. Stir into lima bean mixture until boiling and thickened. Sprinkle with bread crumbs. Serves 4.

1 serving: 182 Calories; 6.7 g Total Fat; 234 mg Sodium; 7 g Protein; 24 g Carbohydrate; 5 g Dietary Fiber

Pictured on page 143.

Vegetables

French Green Bean Fry

Try this recipe the next time you make green beans. Also good with
a sprinkle of grated Cheddar cheese.

Skim evaporated milk	½ cup	125 mL
Cornstarch	1 tbsp.	15 mL
Beef bouillon powder	1 tsp.	5 mL
White (or alcohol-free white) wine	3 tbsp.	50 mL
Ground nutmeg	⅛ tsp.	0.5 mL
Salt	1 tsp.	5 mL
Pepper	¼ tsp.	1 mL
Cooking oil	2 tbsp.	30 mL
Frozen french cut green beans	1 lb.	454 g
Finely chopped onion	½ cup	125 mL
Chopped fresh mushrooms	1 cup	250 mL
Garlic clove, minced (or ¼ tsp., 1 mL, powder)	1	1
Slivered almonds	¼ cup	60 mL

Stir evaporated milk into cornstarch in small bowl. Add next 5 ingredients. Stir. Set aside.

Heat wok or frying pan on medium-high. Add cooking oil. Add frozen green beans, onion, mushrooms, garlic and almonds. Stir-fry for 3 to 4 minutes until tender-crisp. Stir cornstarch mixture. Stir into green bean mixture until boiling and thickened. Makes 4 cups (1 L). Serves 6.

1 serving: 136 Calories; 8 g Total Fat; 585 mg Sodium; 5 g Protein; 12 g Carbohydrate; 3 g Dietary Fiber

Stir-Fry Cabbage

Cooked cabbage in half the time of boiling!

Cooking oil	1 tbsp.	15 mL
Small head of cabbage, coarsely chopped (about 1 lb., 454 g)	6 cups	1.5 L
Salt	¼ tsp.	1 mL
Pepper	⅛ tsp.	0.5 mL
Light sour cream (or more to taste)	¼ cup	60 mL

Heat wok or frying pan on medium-high. Add cooking oil. Add cabbage. Stir-fry for about 2 minutes until tender-crisp, not wilted.

Sprinkle with salt and pepper. Add sour cream. Stir to mix well. Makes 4 cups (1 L). Serves 4.

1 serving: 74 Calories; 4.8 g Total Fat; 199 mg Sodium; 2 g Protein; 7 g Carbohydrate; 2 g Dietary Fiber

Vegetables

Veggie Rice

Crunchy and bright in color which darkens a bit if you add soy sauce.

Long grain white rice	1 cup	250 mL
Chicken bouillon powder	1 tbsp.	15 mL
Water	2 cups	500 mL
Cooking oil	1 tbsp.	15 mL
Water	2 tbsp.	30 mL
Thinly sliced carrot	1 cup	250 mL
Medium green pepper, slivered	1	1
Slivered onion	½ cup	125 mL
Sliced fresh mushrooms	1½ cups	375 mL
Green onions, sliced	2	2
Garlic powder	⅛ tsp.	0.5 mL
Slivered almonds	⅓ cup	75 mL
Low-sodium soy sauce (optional)	1 tbsp.	15 mL

Cook rice in bouillon powder and first amount of water in medium covered saucepan for 15 to 20 minutes until tender and moisture is absorbed. Cover to keep warm.

Heat wok or frying pan on medium high. Add cooking oil and second amount of water. Add carrot. Cover. Steam for 2 minutes. Uncover. Stir-fry for 1 minute.

Add green pepper and onion. Stir-fry for 1 minute.

Add mushrooms, green onion, garlic powder and almonds. Stir-fry until vegetables are tender-crisp.

Stir in rice and soy sauce. Serve immediately. Makes 4 cups (1 L). Serves 4.

1 serving: 319 Calories; 10.5 g Total Fat; 504 mg Sodium; 7 g Protein; 50 g Carbohydrate; 4 g Dietary Fiber

---

Paré Pointer

Children really brighten a home. It seems they don't know how to turn off the lights!

Mushroom Stir-Fry

An excellent mushroom dish with the unusual addition of cucumber.

Chicken bouillon cube	1	1
Boiling water	1/3 cup	75 mL
Cooking oil	1 tbsp.	15 mL
Sliced fresh mushrooms	4 cups	1 L
Cooking oil	1 tbsp.	15 mL
Small English cucumber, with peel, cut into thin strips	1	1
Thinly sliced red onion	1 cup	250 mL
Salt	1/4 tsp.	1 mL
Pepper	1/8 tsp.	0.5 mL
All-purpose flour	1 tbsp.	15 mL
Light sour cream	1/4 cup	60 mL
Green onions, chopped	2	2
Ketchup	1 tsp.	5 mL
Sherry (or alcohol-free sherry)	1 tsp.	5 mL

Dissolve bouillon cube in boiling water in small bowl. Set aside.

Heat wok or frying pan on medium-high. Add first amount of cooking oil. Add mushrooms. Stir-fry for about 3 minutes until golden. Transfer to bowl.

Add second amount of cooking oil to hot wok. Add cucumber and red onion. Stir-fry until soft. Sprinkle with salt and pepper. Add mushrooms.

Sprinkle with flour. Stir to mix. Add sour cream, green onion, ketchup and sherry. Stir bouillon mixture into mushroom mixture until boiling and heated through. Serves 6.

1 serving: 91 Calories; 5.8 g Total Fat; 553 mg Sodium; 2 g Protein; 9 g Carbohydrate; 2 g Dietary Fiber

 Line up ingredients on the counter in the order they are to be added to the wok or frying pan. See page 8 for a guide to cooking times for vegetables.

Vegetables

Shrimp Fried Rice

A bit more special with the addition of peas and green onion.

Cooking oil	1 tbsp.	15 mL
Water	1/4 cup	60 mL
Low-sodium soy sauce	1 tbsp.	15 mL
Seasoned salt	1/2 tsp.	2 mL
Salt	1/4 tsp.	1 mL
Pepper	1/16 tsp.	0.5 mL
Green onions, cut into 1 inch (2.5 cm) lengths	3	3
Granulated sugar	1 tsp.	5 mL
Chicken bouillon powder	1 tsp.	5 mL
Frozen cooked small shrimp, thawed under cold running water	3/4 lb.	340 g
Cooking oil	1 tbsp.	15 mL
Large eggs, fork-beaten	3	3
Frozen peas, thawed	1 cup	250 mL
Cooked rice (about 1 cup, 250 mL, uncooked)	3 cups	750 mL

Combine first 9 ingredients in small bowl. Set aside.

Pat shrimp dry with paper towels.

Heat wok or frying pan on medium-high. Add second amount of cooking oil. Add eggs. Stir-fry until just starting to firm. Add shrimp and peas. Stir-fry until eggs are set. Transfer to bowl.

Add soy sauce mixture to hot wok. Add rice. Stir-fry, breaking up rice, to heat. Add shrimp mixture. Stir to heat through. Serves 4.

1 serving: 457 Calories; 12.9 g Total Fat; 878 mg Sodium; 29 g Protein; 54 g Carbohydrate; 2 g Dietary Fiber

Paré Pointer

Why are kids put to bed wide awake and gotten up when they are sleepy?

Potato Dumplings

Dumplings with a spicy nip. Potatoes need to be prepared the day before for best results.

Potatoes (about 3 medium), peeled and diced	1 lb.	454 g
Water, 1 inch (2.5 cm) deep		
Large egg, fork-beaten	1	1
Salt	½ tsp.	2 mL
Pepper	⅛ tsp.	0.5 mL
All-purpose flour	¾ cup	175 mL
Small croutons (or 8 small cubes of ham)	24	24
Water	6 cups	1.5 L
Salt	¾ tsp.	4 mL

Cook potato in first amount of water in medium saucepan until tender. Drain. Mash. Should make about 1¼ cups (425 mL). Cool. Refrigerate until next day. Freshly cooked potatoes can cause dumplings to fall apart easily.

Mix egg, first amount of salt, pepper and flour into potato. Measure into ¼ cup (60 mL) portions.

Flatten each portion slightly. Shape around 3 croutons or 1 cube of ham.

Bring second amounts of water and salt to a boil in wok on medium-high. Drop potato balls into water in single layer. Simmer slowly, uncovered, for about 10 minutes. Remove dumplings with slotted spoon. Makes 8.

1 dumpling: 99 Calories; 0.8 g Total Fat; 440 mg Sodium; 3 g Protein; 20 g Carbohydrate; 1 g Dietary Fiber

Paré Pointer
Does a goose come from a gooseberry bush?

Ham And Corn Fritters

Everyone will be tempted to overindulge when you make these!

All-purpose flour	½ cup	125 mL
Baking powder	2 tsp.	10 mL
Pepper	¹⁄₁₆ tsp.	0.5 mL
Large eggs, fork-beaten	3	3
Canned kernel corn, drained	12 oz.	341 mL
Canned flakes of ham, drained and broken up	6½ oz.	184 g
Cooking oil, for deep-frying	3 cups	750 mL

Stir flour, baking powder and pepper in medium bowl. Add eggs. Beat in with spoon. Add corn and ham. Mix.

Heat cooking oil in wok on medium-high until 375°F (190°C). Drop batter by rounded teaspoonfuls into hot oil. Deep-fry until browned on all sides. Makes 28.

2 fritters: 94 Calories; 5.3 g Total Fat; 242 mg Sodium; 4 g Protein; 7 g Carbohydrate; 1 g Dietary Fiber

Variation: Drop batter by rounded teaspoonfuls into fine dry bread crumbs. Spoon bread crumbs over top. Deep-fry. These are darker in color.

Corn Fritters

Try these plain, then with ketchup and then with jam.

All-purpose flour	1 cup	250 mL
Baking powder	1 tsp.	5 mL
Salt	1 tsp.	5 mL
Large eggs	2	2
Water (or milk)	3 tbsp.	50 mL
Canned kernel corn, drained	12 oz.	341 mL
Cooking oil, for deep-frying	3 cups	750 mL

Stir flour, baking powder and salt in medium bowl.

Beat eggs in small bowl. Beat in water. Pour into flour mixture. Add corn. Mix well.

Heat cooking oil in wok on medium-high until 375°F (190°C). Drop batter by rounded teaspoonfuls into hot oil. Brown all sides for 3 to 4 minutes. Makes 30.

2 fritters: 69 Calories; 2.4 g Total Fat; 234 mg Sodium; 2 g Protein; 10 g Carbohydrate; 1 g Dietary Fiber

Sauced Fried Fish

Rice wine is used to add flavor to the rice and sauce.

Long grain white rice	1¼ cups	300 mL
Water	2 cups	500 mL
Rice wine	½ cup	125 mL
BATTER		
All-purpose flour	¼ cup	60 mL
Cornstarch	¼ cup	60 mL
Large egg	1	1
Water	3 tbsp.	50 mL
SAUCE		
Hard margarine (or butter)	1 tsp.	5 mL
Green onions, thinly sliced	2	2
Water	¾ cup	175 mL
Cornstarch	2 tsp.	10 mL
Chili sauce	3 tbsp.	50 mL
Brown sugar, packed	1 tsp.	5 mL
Salt	¾ tsp.	4 mL
Garlic powder	¼ tsp.	1 mL
Ground ginger	⅛ tsp.	0.5 mL
Rice wine	1 tbsp.	15 mL
Cooking oil, for deep-frying	3 cups	750 mL
Cod fish fillet, sliced into thin layers	1¼ lbs.	560 g
All-purpose flour	⅓ cup	75 mL

Cook rice in water and rice wine in medium saucepan for 15 to 20 minutes until tender and water is absorbed. Cover to keep warm.

Batter: Mix flour and cornstarch in small bowl.

Beat egg and water in cup. Stir into flour mixture. Add more water if needed to make batter thin enough to coat but not too thin.

Sauce: Heat margarine in small saucepan. Add green onion. Sauté for 1 minute.

Stir water into cornstarch in small bowl. Add next 6 ingredients. Stir. Stir into green onion mixture until boiling and slightly thickened. Keep warm.

(continued on next page)

Wok Deep-Frying

Heat cooking oil in wok on medium-high until 375°F (190°C). Dip fish into flour. Dip into batter to coat. Drop fish into hot oil. Deep-fry until crisp and lightly browned on both sides. Spread rice on 4 individual plates. Divide fish over rice. Spoon sauce over top. Serves 4.

1 serving: 613 Calories; 15.8 g Total Fat; 792 mg Sodium; 33 g Protein; 76 g Carbohydrate; 2 g Dietary Fiber

Beef Meatballs

Serve these zesty little appetizers with cocktail picks.

Milk (or water)	⅓ cup	75 mL
Fine dry bread crumbs	⅓ cup	75 mL
Finely chopped onion	¼ cup	60 mL
Garlic cloves, minced (or ¾ tsp., 4 mL, powder)	3	3
Onion powder	¾ tsp.	4 mL
Salt	¾ tsp.	4 mL
Pepper	¼ tsp.	1 mL
Lean ground beef	1 lb.	454 g
Cornstarch	¼ cup	60 mL
Cooking oil, for deep-frying	3 cups	750 mL

Stir milk, bread crumbs, onion, garlic, onion powder, salt and pepper together in medium bowl.

Add ground beef. Mix. Shape into 1 inch (2.5 cm) balls. Roll in cornstarch to coat.

Heat cooking oil in wok on medium-high until 375°F (190°C). Drop meatballs, a few at a time, into hot oil. Brown well for 3 to 4 minutes. Makes 40.

2 meatballs: 79 Calories; 4.9 g Total Fat; 133 mg Sodium; 5 g Protein; 4 g Carbohydrate; trace Dietary Fiber

Paré Pointer

The car with the wooden engine and the wooden wheels, wooden go!

Bread Dumplings

Woks are the perfect appliance to use for making bread dumplings.

Hard margarine (butter browns too fast)	1 tbsp.	15 mL
Finely chopped onion	½ cup	125 mL
Milk	1 cup	250 mL
Stale bread rolls, cut into ½ inch (12 mm) cubes (see Note)	4½ cups	1.1 L
Large eggs, fork-beaten	2	2
Parsley flakes	½ tsp.	2 mL
Ground nutmeg	¼ tsp.	1 mL
Salt	¼ tsp.	1 mL
Pepper	¼ tsp.	1 mL
All-purpose flour	⅓ cup	75 mL
Water	8 cups	2 L
Salt	1 tsp.	5 mL

Melt margarine in medium saucepan. Add onion. Sauté until soft.

Add milk. Heat until hot but not boiling. Remove from heat. Add bread cubes. Press into milk mixture to soak.

Add next 6 ingredients. Mix well. Using about ¼ cup (60 mL) each, shape into 8 balls.

Heat water and second amount of salt in wok on medium-high until boiling. Drop balls into boiling water, a few at a time. Return water to a boil. Simmer slowly, uncovered, for 15 to 20 minutes until dumplings float. Remove with slotted spoon. Makes 8.

1 dumpling: 151 Calories; 4 g Total Fat; 637 mg Sodium; 6 g Protein; 22 g Carbohydrate; 1 g Dietary Fiber

Note: Cook 1 dumpling first. If it breaks apart, add more bread cubes. If it is too solid, add more milk.

Paré Pointer

An octopus goes into battle fully armed.

Spring Rolls

Tasty little envelopes. Serve with Plum Sauce, page 114.

Cooking oil	1 tbsp.	15 mL
Pork loin (or tenderloin), very finely slivered	6 oz.	170 g
Finely chopped celery	½ cup	125 mL
Finely shredded cabbage	2 cups	500 mL
Cooking oil	1 tbsp.	15 mL
Fresh raw shrimp, peeled and deveined	6 oz.	170 g
Green onions, chopped	3	3
Granulated sugar	1 tsp.	5 mL
Salt	¾ tsp.	4 mL
Pepper	⅛ tsp.	0.5 mL
Egg roll wrappers (4 × 4 inch, 10 × 10 cm, size)	22	22
Large egg, fork-beaten	1	1
Cooking oil, for deep-frying	4 cups	1 L

Heat wok or frying pan on medium-high. Add first amount of cooking oil. Add pork, celery and cabbage. Stir-fry until no pink remains in pork and cabbage is wilted. Transfer to bowl.

Add second amount of cooking oil to hot wok. Add shrimp, green onion, sugar, salt and pepper. Stir-fry until shrimp is pinkish and curled. Remove. Chop. Add to bowl. Stir.

Place rounded tablespoonful of mixture close to corner of wrapper. Fold corner up over filling, tucking under filling. Fold ends in over center. Roll up, making an envelope. Moisten sides of last corner with egg. Seal over center. Repeat until all rolls are completed. Let stand for 30 minutes.

Heat cooking oil in wok on medium-high until 375°F (190°C). Deep-fry spring rolls, a few at a time, in hot oil for about 4 minutes, browning both sides. Drain on paper towel-lined tray in 200°F (95°C) oven. Makes 22.

2 spring rolls: 103 Calories; 6.2 g Total Fat; 148 mg Sodium; 8 g Protein; 4 g Carbohydrate; trace Dietary Fiber

Pictured on page 71.

Egg Rolls: Place ⅛ mixture on each of eight full size 8 × 8 inch (20 × 20 cm) egg roll wrappers. Finish as for Spring Rolls. Makes 8.

Chicken Munchies

Lots of variations. Try all of them so you can pick a favorite.
A bit fussy to make—but delicious!

Water	⅓ cup	75 mL
Cracker crumbs	⅓ cup	75 mL
Salt	½ tsp.	2 mL
Pepper	⅛ tsp.	0.5 mL
Poultry seasoning	¹⁄₁₆ tsp.	0.5 mL
Celery salt	⅛ tsp.	0.5 mL
Onion powder	¼ tsp.	1 mL
Ground chicken	1 lb.	454 g
Cooking oil, for deep-frying	3 cups	750 mL

Stir first 7 ingredients in medium bowl.

Add ground chicken. Mix well. Shape into 1 inch (2.5 cm) balls.

Heat cooking oil in wok on medium-high until 375°F (190°C). Deep-fry chicken balls in hot oil for 1½ minutes until cooked. Makes 40.

2 chicken balls: 44 Calories; 2.3 g Total Fat; 108 mg Sodium; 5 g Protein; 1 g Carbohydrate; trace Dietary Fiber

Taco Chicken Munchies: Add 2 tsp. (10 mL) taco seasoning. Gives a real lift.

Parmesan Chicken Munchies: Roll balls in grated Parmesan cheese. Gives a crispier coating.

Pork Munchies: Omit chicken. Add 1 lb. (454 g) lean ground pork.

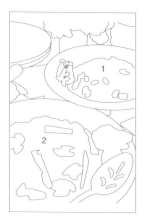

1. Lima Beans And Mushrooms, page 131
2. Carrots And Cabbage, page 130

Props Courtesy Of: Eaton's
　　　　　　　　　Stokes
　　　　　　　　　X/S Wares

Wok Deep-Frying

Deep-Fried Shrimp Meal

Try this instead of the common Fish And Chips. A pleasant change.

Broccoli florets	2 cups	500 mL
Zucchini slices, with peel, dipped into flour	2 cups	500 mL
Small fresh mushrooms	2 cups	500 mL
Fresh raw medium shrimp, peeled and deveined, tails intact	¾ lb.	340 g
BATTER		
Pancake mix	1¼ cups	300 mL
Water	1¼ cups	300 mL
Fine dry bread crumbs	1 cup	250 mL
Cooking oil, for deep-frying	3 cups	750 mL

Have vegetables in large bowl. Arrange shrimp on plate.

Batter: Stir pancake mix and water in small bowl. Dip vegetables and shrimp, 1 piece at a time, into batter to coat.

Roll in bread crumbs. Heat cooking oil in wok on medium-high until 375°F (190°C). Deep-fry several pieces at a time until golden. Remove to paper towel-lined tray in 200°F (95°C) oven to keep warm. Serves 4.

1 serving: 475 Calories; 13.2 g Total Fat; 993 mg Sodium; 28 g Protein; 62 g Carbohydrate; 5 g Dietary Fiber

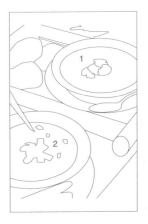

1. Zucchini Chowder, page 148
2. Tortilla Soup, page 146

Props Courtesy Of: Eaton's
The Bay
X/S Wares

Tortilla Soup

A great soup with a just-right taste. Serve immediately so the tortilla strips don't get too soggy.

Cooking oil	1 tbsp.	15 mL
Medium onion, chopped	1	1
Medium green pepper, chopped	1	1
Garlic clove, minced (or ¼ tsp., 1 mL, powder)	1	1
Canned diced tomatoes, with juice	14 oz.	398 mL
Condensed chicken broth	10 oz.	284 mL
Soup can of water	10 oz.	284 mL
Granulated sugar	½ tsp.	2 mL
Salt	½ tsp.	2 mL
Corn tortillas, cut into 2 x ¼ inch (5 cm x 6 mm) strips, for garnish	2	2
Grated Monterey Jack (or sharp Cheddar) cheese, for garnish	¼ cup	60 mL

Heat wok on medium-high. Add cooking oil. Add onion, green pepper and garlic. Stir-fry until onion is soft.

Add tomatoes with juice, chicken broth, water, sugar and salt. Bring mixture to a boil, stirring occasionally. Simmer for 20 minutes.

Divide tortilla strips and cheese among 4 individual bowls. Ladle soup over top. Makes 4 cups (1 L). Serves 4.

1 serving: 92 Calories; 4.6 g Total Fat; 821 mg Sodium; 5 g Protein; 9 g Carbohydrate; 2 g Dietary Fiber

Pictured on page 144.

Chicken Soup

So colorful with carrots and celery showing through.

Cooking oil	1 tbsp.	15 mL
Medium onion, chopped	1	1
Boneless, skinless chicken breast halves (about 2), diced	½ lb.	225 g
Medium potatoes, diced	2	2
Sliced celery	¾ cup	175 mL
Medium carrots, thinly sliced	2	2
Leek (white part only), chopped	1	1

(continued on next page)

Wok Soups

Water	6 cups	1.5 L
Chicken bouillon powder	2 tbsp.	30 mL
Parsley flakes	½ tsp.	2 mL
Salt	½ tsp.	2 mL
Pepper	¹⁄₁₆ tsp.	0.5 mL

Heat wok on medium-high. Add cooking oil. Add onion and chicken. Stir-fry until onion is golden and chicken is cooked.

Add potato, celery, carrot and leeks. Stir. Cover. Simmer for 5 minutes.

Add water, bouillon powder, parsley, salt and pepper. Simmer for 30 minutes. Makes 6 cups (1.5 L). Serves 6.

1 serving: 134 Calories; 3.5 g Total Fat; 931 mg Sodium; 11 g Protein; 15 g Carbohydrate; 2 g Dietary Fiber

---

Split Pea Soup

Make this traditional soup in a wok. Serve with a sprinkle of bacon bits.

Cooking oil	1 tbsp.	15 mL
Medium onion, chopped	1	1
Medium carrot, grated	1	1
Diced celery	½ cup	125 mL
Water	7 cups	1.75 L
Dried split green peas	1½ cups	375 mL
Diced ham (10 oz., 285 g)	1¾ cups	425 mL
Salt	2 tsp.	10 mL
Pepper	½ tsp.	2 mL
Liquid smoke	⅛ tsp.	0.5 mL

Bacon bits, sprinkle

Heat wok on medium-high. Add cooking oil. Add onion, carrot and celery. Stir-fry until vegetables are soft.

Add water and split peas. Simmer, stirring occasionally, until mixture boils. Cover. Simmer for about 1 hour. Process in blender in batches. Return to hot wok.

Add ham, salt, pepper and liquid smoke. Simmer for 5 minutes, stirring often.

Sprinkle with bacon bits. Makes 7 cups (1.75 L). Serves 6.

1 serving: 151 Calories; 7.5 g Total Fat; 1586 mg Sodium; 11 g Protein; 10 g Carbohydrate; 3 g Dietary Fiber

Black Bean Soup

Don't let the color turn you off. The flavor is worth it!

Bacon slices, diced	3	3
Chopped onion	1 cup	250 mL
Medium green pepper, chopped	1	1
Canned black beans, with liquid	19 oz.	540 mL
Water	1 cup	250 mL
Dried whole oregano	1/4 tsp.	1 mL
Salt	1/2 tsp.	2 mL
Pepper	1/8 tsp.	0.5 mL
Chicken bouillon powder	4 tsp.	20 mL
Water	2 cups	500 mL
Chopped ham	1/2 cup	125 mL

Heat wok on medium-high. Stir-fry bacon in wok until cooked. Transfer to bowl.

Add onion and green pepper. Stir-fry until vegetables are soft. Transfer to blender. Add black beans with liquid and first amount of water. Process until smooth. Pour into hot wok.

Stir in next 5 ingredients. Simmer for 5 minutes.

Add ham and bacon. Simmer for 1 minute. Makes 5 cups (1.25 L). Serves 4.

1 serving: 305 Calories; 16.7 g Total Fat; 1729 mg Sodium; 15 g Protein; 24 g Carbohydrate; 4 g Dietary Fiber

Zucchini Chowder

Thick and rich. Yellow base with flecks of green and orange.

Cooking oil	1 tbsp.	15 mL
Grated zucchini, with peel (about 2 medium)	2 1/2 cups	625 mL
Medium carrots, grated	2	2
Medium onion, chopped	1	1
Milk	1 cup	250 mL
All-purpose flour	1/4 cup	60 mL
Condensed chicken broth	2 x 10 oz.	2 x 284 mL
Salt	1/2 tsp.	2 mL
Pepper	1/4 tsp.	1 mL
Grated Monterey Jack cheese	1 cup	250 mL

(continued on next page)

Wok Soups

Heat wok on medium-high. Add cooking oil. Add zucchini, carrot and onion. Stir-fry until vegetables are soft but not brown.

Stir milk into flour in small bowl until smooth. Stir into zucchini mixture. Add chicken broth, salt and pepper. Stir until boiling and thickened.

Add cheese. Stir until melted. Makes 6 cups (1.5 L). Serves 6.

1 serving: 211 Calories; 12.4 g Total Fat; 995 mg Sodium; 12 g Protein; 13 g Carbohydrate; 2 g Dietary Fiber

Pictured on page 144.

Beef Vegetable Soup

Very meaty and brimming with flavor. Makes a big batch.

Cooking oil	1 tsp.	5 mL
Lean ground beef	1 lb.	454 g
Chopped onion	1 cup	250 mL
Cooking oil	1 tsp.	5 mL
Chopped celery	¾ cup	175 mL
Thinly sliced carrot	1¼ cups	300 mL
Chopped cabbage	1½ cups	375 mL
Water	7 cups	1.75 L
Canned diced tomatoes, with juice	14 oz.	398 mL
Dried sweet basil	1 tsp.	5 mL
Chili powder	½ tsp.	2 mL
Salt	1 tsp.	5 mL
Pepper	½ tsp.	2 mL
Granulated sugar	1 tsp.	5 mL
Worcestershire sauce	1 tsp.	5 mL
Beef bouillon powder	3 tbsp.	50 mL

Heat wok on medium-high. Add first amount of cooking oil. Add ground beef and onion. Stir-fry until beef is no longer pink. Drain. Transfer to bowl.

Add second amount of cooking oil to hot wok. Add celery, carrot and cabbage. Stir-fry until tender-crisp. Add beef mixture.

Add remaining 9 ingredients. Bring mixture to a boil, stirring occasionally. Cover. Simmer for 30 minutes. Makes 10 cups (2.5 L). Serves 8.

1 serving: 150 Calories; 7.6 g Total Fat; 1141 mg Sodium; 12 g Protein; 8 g Carbohydrate; 2 g Dietary Fiber

Minestrone

Has a nice zing. A hearty soup for hearty appetites.

Cooking oil	1 tsp.	5 mL
Lean ground beef	1 lb.	454 g
Medium onion, chopped	1	1
Cooking oil	2 tsp.	10 mL
Diced carrot	⅔ cup	150 mL
Diced potato	1 cup	250 mL
Finely chopped cabbage	1 cup	250 mL
Diced celery	½ cup	125 mL
Canned kidney beans, with liquid	14 oz.	398 mL
Canned crushed tomatoes	14 oz.	398 mL
Water	6 cups	1.5 L
Worcestershire sauce	2 tbsp.	30 mL
Beef bouillon powder	3 tbsp.	50 mL
Uncooked elbow macaroni	1 cup	250 mL
Parsley flakes	1 tsp.	5 mL
Garlic powder	½ tsp.	2 mL
Salt	1 tsp.	5 mL
Pepper	¼ tsp.	1 mL
Granulated sugar	1 tsp.	5 mL

Grated Parmesan cheese, sprinkle

Heat wok on medium-high. Add first amount of cooking oil. Add ground beef and onion. Stir-fry for 4 to 5 minutes until beef is no longer pink. Drain.

Add second amount of cooking oil to hot wok. Add carrot, potato, cabbage and celery. Stir-fry for 3 minutes.

Add kidney beans with liquid, tomatoes, water, Worcestershire sauce and bouillon powder. Stir. Bring mixture to a boil. Boil for 20 minutes.

Add next 6 ingredients. Cover. Simmer for 20 minutes until macaroni is tender but firm.

Sprinkle individual servings with Parmesan cheese. Makes 9 cups (2.25 L). Serves 8.

1 serving: 226 Calories; 5.6 g Total Fat; 1239 mg Sodium; 17 g Protein; 27 g Carbohydrate; 4 g Dietary Fiber

Wok Soups

Measurement Tables

Throughout this book measurements are given in Conventional and Metric measure. To compensate for differences between the two measurements due to rounding, a full metric measure is not always used. The cup used is the standard 8 fluid ounce. Temperature is given in degrees Fahrenheit and Celsius. Baking pan measurements are in inches and centimetres as well as quarts and litres. An exact metric conversion is given below as well as the working equivalent (Standard Measure).

Spoons

Conventional Measure	Metric Exact Conversion Millilitre (mL)	Metric Standard Measure Millilitre (mL)
1/8 teaspoon (tsp.)	0.6 mL	0.5 mL
1/4 teaspoon (tsp.)	1.2 mL	1 mL
1/2 teaspoon (tsp.)	2.4 mL	2 mL
1 teaspoon (tsp.)	4.7 mL	5 mL
2 teaspoons (tsp.)	9.4 mL	10 mL
1 tablespoon (tbsp.)	14.2 mL	15 mL

Cups

Conventional Measure	Metric Exact Conversion Millilitre (mL)	Metric Standard Measure Millilitre (mL)
1/4 cup (4 tbsp.)	56.8 mL	60 mL
1/3 cup (5 1/3 tbsp.)	75.6 mL	75 mL
1/2 cup (8 tbsp.)	113.7 mL	125 mL
2/3 cup (10 2/3 tbsp.)	151.2 mL	150 mL
3/4 cup (12 tbsp.)	170.5 mL	175 mL
1 cup (16 tbsp.)	227.3 mL	250 mL
4 1/2 cups	1022.9 mL	1000 mL (1 L)

Oven Temperatures

Fahrenheit (°F)	Celsius (°C)
175°	80°
200°	95°
225°	110°
250°	120°
275°	140°
300°	150°
325°	160°
350°	175°
375°	190°
400°	205°
425°	220°
450°	230°
475°	240°
500°	260°

Dry Measurements

Conventional Measure Ounces (oz.)	Metric Exact Conversion Grams (g)	Metric Standard Measure Grams (g)
1 oz.	28.3 g	28 g
2 oz.	56.7 g	57 g
3 oz.	85.0 g	85 g
4 oz.	113.4 g	125 g
5 oz.	141.7 g	140 g
6 oz.	170.1 g	170 g
7 oz.	198.4 g	200 g
8 oz.	226.8 g	250 g
16 oz.	453.6 g	500 g
32 oz.	907.2 g	1000 g (1 kg)

Pans

Conventional Inches	Metric Centimetres
8x8 inch	20x20 cm
9x9 inch	22x22 cm
9x13 inch	22x33 cm
10x15 inch	25x38 cm
11x17 inch	28x43 cm
8x2 inch round	20x5 cm
9x2 inch round	22x5 cm
10x4 1/2 inch tube	25x11 cm
8x4x3 inch loaf	20x10x7.5 cm
9x5x3 inch loaf	22x12.5x7.5 cm

Casseroles

CANADA & BRITAIN		UNITED STATES	
Standard Size Casserole	Exact Metric Measure	Standard Size Casserole	Exact Metric Measure
1 qt. (5 cups)	1.13L	1 qt. (4 cups)	900 mL
1 1/2 qts. (7 1/2 cups)	1.69 L	1 1/2 qts. (6 cups)	1.35 L
2 qts. (10 cups)	2.25 L	2 qts. (8 cups)	1.8 L
2 1/2 qts. (12 1/2 cups)	2.81 L	2 1/2 qts. (10 cups)	2.25 L
3 qts. (15 cups)	3.38 L	3 qts. (12 cups)	2.7 L
4 qts. (20 cups)	4.5 L	4 qts. (16 cups)	3.6 L
5 qts. (25 cups)	5.63 L	5 qts. (20 cups)	4.5 L

Index

155

156

Company's Coming cookbooks are available at retail locations throughout Canada!

EXCLUSIVE mail order offer on next page

Buy any 2 cookbooks—choose a 3rd FREE of equal or less value than the lowest price paid.

Original Series — CA$15.99 Canada — US$12.99 USA & International

CODE		CODE		CODE	
SQ	150 Delicious Squares	SC	Slow Cooker Recipes	RC	The Rookie Cook
CA	Casseroles	ODM	One-Dish Meals	RHR	Rush-Hour Recipes
MU	Muffins & More	ST	Starters	SW	Sweet Cravings
SA	Salads	SF	Stir-Fry	YRG	Year-Round Grilling
AP	Appetizers	MAM	Make-Ahead Meals	GG	Garden Greens
SS	Soups & Sandwiches	PB	The Potato Book	CHC	Chinese Cooking
CO	Cookies	CCLFC	Low-Fat Cooking	PK	The Pork Book
PA	Pasta	CCLFP	Low-Fat Pasta	RL	Recipes For Leftovers
BA	Barbecues	CFK	Cook For Kids	EB	The Egg Book
PR	Preserves	SCH	Stews, Chilies & Chowders	SDP	School Days Parties
CH	Chicken, Etc.	FD	Fondues	HS	Herbs & Spices
KC	Kids Cooking	CCBE	The Beef Book	BEV	The Beverage Book **NEW**
CT	Cooking For Two	CB	The Cheese Book		*October 1/04*

Lifestyle Series

CODE	CA$17.99 Canada US$15.99 USA & International
DC	Diabetic Cooking

CODE	CA$19.99 Canada US$15.99 USA & International
HC	Heart-Friendly Cooking
DDI	Diabetic Dinners

Most Loved Recipe Collection

CODE	CA$23.99 Canada US$19.99 USA & International
MLA	Most Loved Appetizers
MLMC	Most Loved Main Courses

Special Occasion Series

CODE	CA$20.99 Canada US$19.99 USA & International
GFK	Gifts from the Kitchen

CODE	CA$22.99 Canada US$19.99 USA & International
WC	Weekend Cooking

CODE	CA$24.99 Canada US$19.99 USA & International
BSS	Baking—Simple to Sensational **NEW**
	September 1/04

Company's Coming COOKBOOKS

Company's Coming Publishing Limited
2311 – 96 Street
Edmonton, Alberta, Canada T6N 1G3
Tel: 780-450-6223 Fax: 780-450-1857
www.companyscoming.com

EXCLUSIVE Mail Order Offer

See previous page for list of cookbooks

Buy 2 Get 1 FREE!

Buy any 2 cookbooks—choose a 3rd FREE
of equal or less value than the lowest price paid.

Quantity	Code	Title	Price Each	Price Total
			$	$
TOTAL BOOKS (including FREE)		**TOTAL BOOKS PURCHASED:**	$	

	International	Canada & USA
Plus Shipping & Handling (per destination)	$11.98 (one book)	$5.98 (one book)
Additional Books (including FREE books)	$ ($4.99 each)	$ ($1.99 each)
Sub-Total	$	$
Canadian residents add G.S.T.(7%)		$
TOTAL AMOUNT ENCLOSED	$	$

The Fine Print

- Orders outside Canada must be **PAID IN US FUNDS** by cheque or money order drawn on Canadian or US bank or by credit card.
- Make cheque or money order payable to: **Company's Coming Publishing Limited**.
- Prices are expressed in Canadian dollars for Canada, US dollars for USA & International and are subject to change without prior notice.
- Orders are shipped surface mail. For courier rates, visit our web-site: **www.companyscoming.com** or contact us: Tel: 780-450-6223 Fax: 780-450-1857.
- Sorry, no C.O.D.'s.

☐ MasterCard   ☐ VISA

_____ Expiry date

Account # _____

Name of cardholder _____

Cardholder's signature _____

Gift Giving

- Let us help you with your gift giving!
- We will send cookbooks directly to the recipients of your choice if you give us their names and addresses.
- Please specify the titles you wish to send to each person.
- If you would like to include your personal note or card, we will be pleased to enclose it with your gift order.
- Company's Coming Cookbooks make excellent gifts: Birthdays, bridal showers, Mother's Day, Father's Day, graduation or any occasion …collect them all!

Shipping Address

Send the cookbooks listed above to:

Name: _____

Street: _____

City: _____ Prov./State: _____

Country: _____ Postal Code/Zip: _____

Tel: ( ) _____

Email address: _____

☐ YES! Please send a catalogue

Boost your breakfast with something cold and fruity or pour something warm and relaxing after supper. *The Beverage Book* is perfect for everyday fare or entertaining family and friends.

In this book:
- Breakfast Drinks
- Coffee & Tea Drinks
- Frozen & Juicer Drinks
- Holiday & Theme Drinks
- Punches & Pitcher Drinks
- Kids' Drinks & more!

Company's Coming
COOKBOOKS®

Quick
&
Easy
Recipes

Everyday
Ingredients

Canada's
most popular
cookbooks!